HAIL! FULL OF GRACE

Simple Thoughts on the Rosary

by

Mother Mary Loyola

Edited by
Rev. Herbert Thurston, S.J.

2015
St. Augustine Academy Press
Homer Glen, Illinois

This book is newly typeset based on the fourth edition published in 1906 by B. Herder. All editing strictly limited to the correction of errors in the original text and minor clarifications in punctuation or phrasing. Any remaining oddities of spelling or phrasing are as found in the original.

Nihil Obstat
HERBERT THURSTON, S.J.
Censor Deputatus

Imprimatur
HERBERTUS CARD. VAUGHAN
Archiep. Westmonast.

This book was originally published in 1902 by Sands & Co.
This edition ©2011 by St. Augustine Academy Press.
All editing by Lisa Bergman.

Second Printing September 2015

ISBN: 978-1-936639-03-8
Library of Congress Control Number: 2011941817

Unless otherwise noted, all illustrations in this book, including the cover, are either the original illustrations as found in the book, or are public domain images.

Frontispiece Illustration:
Holy Card Heaven. http://holycardheaven.blogspot.com, October 22, 2010.

"**Catholic literature,** doctrinal and devotional, owes a great deal to Mother Mary Loyola. There is a certain wholesomeness, naturalness, geniality about her spirituality that at once wins a place in the Catholic heart for whatever she writes." —The Ecclesiastical Review, volume 58, January 1918

About Mother Mary Loyola:

Most Catholics today who have heard the name Mother Mary Loyola know her as the author of *The King of the Golden City*, which has enjoyed a resurgence in popularity in recent years. But few know that she wrote over two dozen works, and that she was once a household name among Catholics of her era. What made her unique among Catholic authors was her ability to draw in her listeners with story after story—and not just any stories, but ones that incorporated current events and brand new inventions of the time. Despite the fact that those events are no longer current, and those inventions no longer brand new, her books scintillate with the appeal of an active mind that could find a moral in the most unusual places. And while the printed word lacks the animated facial expressions and vocal inflections which reveal a gifted storyteller, hers convey her enthusiasm so capably that the reader can easily imagine sitting at the feet of this wise old nun.

About *Hail! Full of Grace*:

In *Hail! Full of Grace*, Mother Loyola brings her full talent for storytelling to bear on the fifteen mysteries of the Rosary. Like a tourguide to the Holy Land, she brings the reader along on a journey through the lives of our Lord and of his Blessed Mother. We experience, through her vivid illustration, the breathless anticipation, the drudgery and hardship, the depths of sorrow and despair, and the heights of joy unimaginable. No detail escapes her notice as she travels on, until her readers feel less that they have meditated upon the mysteries of the Rosary, and rather more that they have experienced them firsthand.

To learn more about Mother Mary Loyola, visit our website at
www.staugustineacademypress.com.

TO MARY IMMACULATE

OUR LIFE

OUR SWEETNESS

AND OUR HOPE

Contents

	PAGE
Preface	ix
Introduction	xiv

I. The Joyful Mysteries

The Annunciation	1
The Visitation	8
The Nativity	15
The Presentation	24
The Finding in the Temple	34

II. The Sorrowful Mysteries

Mary and the Passion	42
The Agony in the Garden	46
The Scourging at the Pillar	60
The Crowning with Thorns	67
The Carrying of the Cross	76
The Crucifixion	89

III. The Glorious Mysteries

The Resurrection	114
The Ascension	141
The Descent of the Holy Ghost	158
The Assumption of the Blessed Virgin	171
The Coronation of the Blessed Virgin	186

Editor's Note:

In presenting this edition, I have attempted to be as faithful as possible to the original text of Mother Mary Loyola's *Hail! Full of Grace* as printed by B. Herder in 1906. Though I strongly considered making editorial changes in order to improve grammar or punctuation, I avoided doing so in all but the most egregious cases, in order to present to you, the reader, exactly what Mother Loyola wrote. Therefore the many idiosyncracies you may find herein are not mistakes, but rather, features of the original.

Lisa Bergman
St. Augustine Academy Press

Preface

It would be hard to find a more striking example of the sure instinct with which the Church feels her way to what is most helpful and practical in matters of piety, than the gradual adoption and final acceptance throughout the Catholic world of the devotion of the Rosary. Whatever difference of opinion may exist regarding the historical question of the origin of this form of prayer, there can be no hesitation in proclaiming it to be singularly adapted to the needs and capacities of the great body of the faithful. It is sometimes disparaged as a mechanical form of devotion, akin to the praying wheel of the Buddhists, and there is sufficient semblance of truth in the reproach to make it sound plausible, but the people who use such language can have little acquaintance with the Rosary as it is practised by those who love it and who understand its possibilities. After all, wherever any constant form of words is employed there is danger that such forms after a while may lose their power to rouse the attention, and may come to be repeated more or less mechanically. Those must, I venture to think, be very exceptional persons, who after long experience of public prayers at night or morning can assure us that the word spoken by the lips never fails to excite the appropriate mental concept. Whether the Our Father be recited once a day or fifty times a day, it is almost equally difficult at any given recitation to follow the complex train of ideas embodied in the sounds which frequent repetition has made so familiar. This is true even for the educated, but it must be much more true in the case of those millions of simple and uninstructed peasant folk, for whose devotional needs it is the Church's special care to provide. Is it not then reasonable that she should accept a more or less mechanical recitation as almost inevitable, and that she should do her best to make profit out of this very difficulty? To tell such persons simply to meditate or to frame prayers for themselves is to show little acquaintance with the very limited capacities of the uneducated multitude. If these are to pray in private they must have something definite to do, something at least to measure by, something to count, something to say. Scientists tell us that there must be a nucleus to form the rain drop, that there must be some foreign body upon which the silver held in solution can be precipitated by an electric discharge. The illiterate cannot commit to memory psalms or long prayers, but given a rudimentary apparatus of Hail Marys, which the very dullest can learn and understand, it is a comparatively easy task to graft upon this stock a system of meditations recalling the incidents of Our Lord's Life. The child or the peasant who would remain vacant-eyed and open-mouthed if bidden to make a mental prayer upon the Nativity of Our Lord, becomes an apt learner enough when we tell him to say ten Hail Marys to Our Lady beside the Crib. There is surely no irreverence in using Hail Marys devoutly repeated as in some sense a measure of time. Though the individual words are little marked, it is fully realised that each is a salutation to Mary. We acknowledge the advent of Royalty with the meaningless discharge of cannon duly numbered. We count by three times three the acclamations with which we hail a popular hero. Why should not Gabriel's salutation be echoed by the faithful on earth, as the "Holy, Holy, Holy," is repeated unceasingly before the presence of the Most High by the choirs of Angels in Heaven? After all there is music in the words. They are the *bourdon* of a melody which each faithful soul, according to the measure of its individual gifts, improvises for itself in contemplating the scenes of Our Saviour's Life and Resurrection. And even where the individual effort is very feeble, who shall say that those bare whispered *Aves* have no appointed place in the chorus of human praise? It must be a most varied harmony which rises heavenwards from a Church which is the Church of the poor as well as of the rich, of the ignorant multitude as well as of the lettered few. There is no more eloquent proof of the Church's divine origin than that she makes provision for all her children and takes account of their very different needs, regardless of quality or station. Let it be added at once that I must not be understood to imply that the Rosary is a devotion intended only for the uneducated. No one who may make acquaintance with the reflexions which Mother Loyola has provided in this little book will fail to see that the Rosary is a form of prayer in which both imagination and intelligence may be exercised to the full. Moreover, everyday experience tells us that there are few educated persons who have become familiar with this devotion who do not discover a certain nameless sweetness in its simple methods. No one need fear that he is too intellectual to find help and consolation in his Rosary, though perhaps for those who have not learned the practice in their youth some little perseverance may be required before the full possibilities of the exercise are appreciated. Probably not the least part of its charm lies in this, that here, master and servant, parents and children, learned and ignorant, cleric and layman meet, and are conscious that they meet, upon common ground.

I have designedly refrained in these few words of preface from making any comment upon the history of the Rosary. But there is one fact as to which all students of our devotional literature must be agreed, and that is that since the close of the fifteenth century the Dominican Order have made it specially their own and have had more to do than any other religious body with the universal adoption of this admirable form of prayer. It is to the innumerable confraternities of the Rosary established under Dominican auspices that we owe the prevalence of the fifteen "mysteries," now so familiar, over all and every other of the many "crowns" and chaplets which disputed the pre-eminence in the early years of the sixteenth century. Neither can any thoughtful person hesitate to recognise the intrinsic superiority of an arrangement which is at once eminently simple and which contains so much of what is certain and scriptural, and so little of what is mere matter of fancy. No devout Catholic, whether instructed or ignorant, who habitually meditates upon the mysteries of the Rosary as our Holy Father has exhorted us all to do, can fail to acquire a very real familiarity with the most vital of those lessons which our Divine Redeemer came from Heaven to teach mankind by His example. Such a one may not follow by any conscious act the meaning of each recurrent phrase in the quickly repeated *Aves*, but he will have learned in what sense Our Lady is full of grace, how far she is privileged above her fellows, how blessed is indeed the fruit of her womb, and this perhaps more thoroughly than if his mind had been slavishly attentive to the exact signification of every uttered word.

Finally, it is in the conviction that it would be difficult to meet with more helpful thoughts, or more vivid pictures than Mother Loyola has here provided to aid us in the meditation of the drama of man's Redemption that I commend the pages which follow to the consideration of all true lovers of Our Lady's Rosary.

HERBERT THURSTON, S.J.
NEUILLY SUR SEINE, 16th Sept. 1902

Introduction

People are coming to understand as they never understood before how much can be learned by the simple act of sight. The eye is an apt scholar, and not only takes in readily, but retains faithfully. Hitherto, however, it has been lazy, or, at any rate, it has not done its fair share of work. Hence a general determination that it shall make up now for lost time. Pictures are multiplied on every side. Our primers and our prayer-books swarm with them. Our magazines are coming to be in great part illustration. Our advertisements are often a picture and a word. In the lecture room the magic lantern is in constant requisition. So thoroughly, indeed, has every one waked up to the fact that a great means of education has been neglected in the past, that there is a danger of our suffering from its excessive use in the future.

Now, the Church found out the value of pictures long ago. She lined her walls with illustrations while she was yet in the catacombs. She carried all over the world the crucifix and the banner of Mary as her first instruction in Christian doctrine. She converted nations by paintings of the Last Judgment. And when the loving saint of Assisi found from his meditations on the Infant Jesus how useful it is to have a scene before us when we pray, She gave us the Christmas crib, which has become a necessity, not only in every Catholic church through out the world, but in the schoolroom and the nursery. By means of Mystery and Miracle Plays the simple folk of this country were taught, as they have never been taught since, to realise Bethlehem, and Nazareth, and Calvary. And the lessons sank deep. The hold that the life of Christ and His Blessed Mother had on imagination and mind and heart in the ages of faith is evidenced, among other ways, by the rhymes then in common use that have been preserved to us in old manuscripts.

Yet pictures to be of any use must be looked at thoughtfully. Watch some people walking through an art gallery in which are gathered together masterpieces of, say, the English school of painting. They move on with the regularity of a machine. Portraits, still life, landscapes, interiors, village scenes, battle, and sea pieces pass in unbroken procession before their eye, which has not the chance of conveying a single distinct impression to the brain. You ask them what they thought of the collection, and will be told: "Oh, it was all very nice!"

Something after this fashion do people look at the Crib and the Crucifix. What wonder, then, if sights that have drawn tears from sinners and from saints have no effect *on them*.

Not so did Mary look. She saw and pondered. She saw the little trembling form in the manger on Christmas night; the face of the Babe on the day of His Presentation; the look in the Boy's eyes when they met hers in the Temple courts. "And Mary kept all these things, pondering them in her heart." Strange to say, it was because she knew so much more and saw so much further than we see, that she took care not to hurry on and miss her lesson. She knelt in adoring love before her little One an hour old, and said to Him: "Wast Thou not from the beginning, O Lord, my God, my Holy One!" (Hab. 1). She looked at Him whose tiny fingers clasped hers so tight, and remembered that He had prepared the heavens and the earth, and compassed the sea with its bounds (Prov. 8). What wonder that her soul was for ever magnifying the Lord, and rejoicing in God her Saviour!

For she knew why all this was done. Long before St. Paul, she had said: "He loved me and delivered Himself for me." It was to get her her wondrous graces, to do great things for her, that He had emptied Himself of His glory and come down upon earth. She could not get used to these thoughts. They never lost their freshness. She gazed and gazed upon Him with untiring love and thankfulness, and ever-growing wonder and delight. And as she gazed, the virtue of the Sacred Humanity went out to her, as later to the needy, suffering crowd. For to look lovingly at Jesus in the mysteries of His human life is to draw into our own lives the virtues of His. The sun prints upon the sensitized plate the image we desire. More wondrously the true Light works upon our souls. But we must give it time. O that we had a little of our Mother's habit of *pondering*; blessed habit, it has made the Church's saints in every age!

In His prayer for His apostles at the Last Supper, our Lord said: "This is eternal life, that they may know Thee, the only true God, and Jesus Christ whom Thou has sent" (John 17). By this knowledge of Himself, to which eternal life is attached, He surely intended no mere barren belief in the divinity of His Person, and in His Mission, but an interior and familiar knowledge akin to theirs who followed Him about during His earthly life, who stood by when He taught in the Temple, and toiled up Calvary, and spoke from the Cross. These sights and sounds were not for His Holy Mother and a few men and women of one generation only, but for His followers in all time. St. John says: "In Him was life, and the life was the light of men…the true light which enlighteneth every man that cometh into this world" (John 1). And St. Paul declares: "We shall be saved by His life" (Romans 5). That divine life is our great exemplar. A certain measure of conformity with it is a necessary condition of salvation. In proportion to their conformity is the eternal happiness of all the elect.

But the lessons of Christ's life on earth, which are as essential to us as the redemption He wrought on Calvary, can only avail us by being diligently pondered. St. Paul speaks of "learning Christ" (Ephes. 4), a phrase implying study. "Learn of Me," our Lord Himself says to us. We must watch, we must listen intently, it we would gain a real insight into the mysteries of the three and thirty years. And by the side of the Son, and for a fuller comprehension of Him, we must contemplate the Mother, the first and most faithful of His disciples, who says to us, with far greater right than St. Paul: "Be ye followers of me, as I am of Christ" (1 Cor. 4). We cannot separate these two lives, the most closely interwoven that earth has ever seen. We cannot study them apart without missing the significance of each. Together they must work their effect upon our souls.

This being so, we might be sure the Church would provide us with a method by which we may draw near to Jesus and Mary, near enough for the purposes of study: and an easy method, within reach of us all. She does not disappoint us. She sees her children in every generation, of every condition in life, under every variety of circumstances, rich and poor, learned and simple, young and old, the toilers and the leisured, the successful and the downtrodden, calling to her to supply their need, and her answer to all is—the Rosary. Here is an easy means of bringing the sacred mysteries of the Incarnation home to us, and of gradually conforming our lives to the likeness of the two perfect lives on which we gaze awhile each day. Hence our Holy Father, Leo XIII., in his Encyclical on the Rosary, says: "Among the several rites of honouring the Blessed Mary, some are to be preferred, inasmuch as we know them to be the most powerful and the most pleasing to our Mother; and therefore do we most specially name and recommend the Rosary, which recalls to our minds the great mysteries of Jesus and Mary—joys, sorrows, and triumphs." And again: "We most earnestly exhort all the faithful to persevere devoutly in the daily recitation of the Rosary" (Leo XIII. *Brev. Salutaris ille*). These are weighty words, and deserve to be considered attentively one by one.

We—the highest authority on earth, the Vicar of Christ, the mouthpiece of the Holy Spirit to the children of the Church, who learn the Will of God and the way of salvation from Our lips:

Most earnestly exhort—that is advocate and counsel with all the authority and solicitude of the pastoral office:

All the faithful—not only priests and religious, the needy, the troubled, the leisured—but *all*—busy men in the professions and trades, students, clerks, toilers in the factory and in the field, the sick, the old, the little children.

To the daily recitation—Does this seem an inconsiderate demand when work is so heavy and repose so short? It might be were the Rosary an additional burden. But the busiest and the most weary will tell you they can find ten minutes for their beads, time to avail themselves for that brief space of our Lord's invitation: "Come aside and rest a little."

And to persevere—It is easy to take up a holy practice. To persevere in it takes courage, generosity, self-sacrifice in a word, a true love of God, and a dogged determination to save one's soul, and to take the best means to that end.

Devoutly—This is harder still, unless we have come to love our Rosary, to say it—if not with sensible fervour, at least with the fervour of the will, i.e., with the reasonable application of mind and heart which is enough to ensure to us its precious fruits.

It is, alas, but too true that many of us find the ten minutes given to our Rosary a sadly weary time. It gets no easier with practice, and we see no reason for believing it is becoming more fruitful.

In the generality of cases the cause of this trouble is not far to seek. The Rosary cannot be well said, cannot be an act of piety, still less can be a pleasure, and an unfailing resource in every need and mood, unless we take some trouble to say it well. What, then, are we to do? There can be no question of giving it up, of loosening our hold on the chain let down from heaven to draw us in safety thither. The only thing, therefore, to be done is to try to find out why the Rosary is so tedious to us.

Have I a method in saying it? Or, if nothing I can dignify by the name of method, have I, when I turn aside from the sights and sounds of daily life, anything to substitute for them during the few minutes given to my beads? As these pass through my fingers, is every wandering thought allowed free course through my mind? If so, is there any wonder that I find my Rosary neither attractive nor helpful?

To say the Rosary as I ought, two things are requisite—(1) in my exterior deportment the reverence becoming one who is in converse with the Queen of Heaven; (2) reasonable pains to withdraw my mind from irrelevant thoughts, and fix them on one or other aspect of the many-sided mysteries I am contemplating. I should, therefore, try to banish from my mind frivolous or useless recollections, and should seek as far as may be a time and place where objects that would strike my senses and draw my thoughts from the subject I am considering may be shut out. We cannot think of two things at once, and we must get rid of one set of thoughts if we are to make room for another. I must leave as far as possible the scenes of my daily life, and betake myself—with my anxieties and difficulties if I will—to other scenes, where a perfect life was lived for me, and where difficulties and anxieties were perfectly met in order to be my example.

Far-off scenes and persons are made marvellously real to us in these days by means of the cinematograph and the gramophone. We see a train come puffing into a station, the passengers alight, come down the swarming platform, and smile at us as they pass. In a concert room we may hear the very tones of the voice of some famous singer. Little effort is needed to recall the memory of these sights and sounds. Nay, considerable effort is necessary to efface them from the imagination on which they have engraved themselves.

If only we could so bring before our minds the Gospel scenes as to be impressed with something of this sense of reality! And why not? We can familiarise ourselves with the Gospel narrative, put together pictures we have seen, and descriptions we have heard, and in this way create for ourselves a very helpful environment when we come to contemplate an incident in the life of our Lord or of His Blessed Mother. Of course, there cannot be quite the same vividness, and, of course, there must be effort and diligence—what is ever done without? But how can effort be better spent? Little by little our scenes take shape, and at last the very name of a mystery brings before us the picture that will not only help to fix our imagination, but be a source of holy and helpful thoughts.

We *see* the little room at Nazareth, and the child of fourteen at her prayer. We *see* her reverence, her stillness, the Angel coming in. We *hear* his salutation, and listen for her reply. We notice the beautiful virtues that come out in it, and love these virtues more and more for seeing their loveliness in Mary. We *feel*, as it were, the expectancy of heaven and earth in that midnight hour, the most eventful in the world's history. We *see* the cave at Bethlehem, how low and dark it is. We *feel* the prickly straw. We *hear* the few whispered words of Mary and Joseph.

And so in the other mysteries. In all of them we watch our Lord as if we were present and saw Him in the Temple, in the Garden of Gethsemane, on His way to Calvary. We note His attitude, the expression of His face, His words, His silence, His gestures. And through these exterior signs we try to learn what is passing in His Heart. Thus the picturing of the scene leads by a natural transition to the contemplation of persons, words, and actions.

In all this we must not tire the head by over taxing the imagination. The rule here as in all things is, to take what helps and to leave what hinders us. Only, it is well to give the representation of the scene and the dwelling on persons, words, and actions a fair trial. Indeed, it is hard to know what we can substitute for this that is not the same thing—supposing of course we do not limit our attention to the words we are saying. To understand the Rosary as the Church understands it, and as she proposes it to us, we must bear in mind that it is *a study* of Christ and of His Blessed Mother. The study may be no more than a quiet, restful gaze, but even this supposes some such concentration of the mind on persons, or on what they are doing or saying.

It may not be amiss to notice the objection of those who say: "If our pictures were anything better than the creatures of our own brain; if we could bring before us the scenes we wish to contemplate with anything like truth of detail, then indeed they would help; but how few of us can do this." There is some force, perhaps, in this objection, though it did not trouble St. Bernard or St. Bonaventure. Those who find it unsurmountable can only let their brain pictures alone. By far the greater number of us, however, are helped by even an approximation to the truth. When Gustave Doré was at school, his professor of history often made use of his talent for the benefit of his companions. "Doré, step up to the board and draw a portrait of Nero, that these gentlemen may fully understand what I have been saying." Even an imaginative portrait has its value in fixing the attention, as the French professor well knew.

St. Ignatius would have us consider whether the road from Nazareth to Bethlehem "be level or through valleys and over hills: whether the stable or cave of the Nativity be large or small, low or high, and how fitted up." As if the imagination might be left a good deal to its own power of construction. At the same time, it cannot but be praiseworthy to aim at historical accuracy as far as possible. Love delights in detail; the love of God for us, and our love for Him is no exception to this rule.

If a friend leaves the old country and settles in Australia, we must know all about the new home out there—how the house lies, the extent of the ground it covers, its plan, prospect, rooms; above all, his own sanctum, and the place where the greater part of his day is spent. We must have photographs to help out his description. We want to picture him to ourselves. So we put together all the material that comes to hand, and let loving imagination fill up the gaps.

Can it be less interesting to know what the Holy House at Nazareth was like, and the Temple, and the Supper Room on Mount Sion? Surely the chief and noblest work for which our imagination is given is to occupy itself with the mysteries of the God-Man during His life on earth.

Still, there are many who find no help in representing to themselves past and distant scenes. They like to say their Rosary in the actuality of the Real Presence. Choosing an hour when the church is quiet, they take up their position before the tabernacle, and by an act of vivid faith try to realise that He is there who came to Mary, and hung in agony, and rose in glory.

But in whatever way we strive to bring home to us the mysteries of our Lord's life, let us bear in mind that our study is no mere head exercise. The head works only for the sake of the heart and the will. We look and learn with a view to practice, remembering that our Lord did, or said, or suffered this or that, with us in His mind, and on purpose for us. The thought uppermost in our mind must be—*all this for me*. We have such a way of thinking of our Lord's life as a piece of New Testament history that was a great deal to John and Magdalen, who listened to His words, and stood under the Cross; but as not concerning us individually, not concerning *me*. Whereas it was for me as well as for Mary Magdalen that he said "Thy sins are forgiven thee." As much for me as for John that He said to His Holy Mother—"Behold thy son." We lose what our Lord meant us to gain by the story of His life, unless we remember that we individually were present to Him in all the Gospel scenes, and that it was because our needs had to be provided for, that He spoke and acted as we read.

In a certain connoisseur's collection of paintings is a very old picture of the Crucifixion. It is not beautiful, but it is striking. The canvas is cracked, the figures are stiff, the colours are hard and dull. Our Lady is there and Magdalen and John. And kneeling at the foot of the Cross, is a nun looking up at our Lord, whose face is turned to her. The picture has a curious story. The nun was the abbess of a certain convent and a friend of the artist. Hearing he was going to paint the Crucifixion, she said to him—"Oh! do put me in. I was really there, you know. Our Lord had me in His mind when He hung on the Cross. He saw me. He spoke to me; do put me in." The picture may not be more interesting to others for her presence there, but to herself it must certainly have made the Crucifixion, and the death of her Saviour *for her*, a fact more vividly realised. Let us do for ourselves what no artist is likely to do for us—put ourselves into the scene whenever we look at Calvary or any other scene of our Lord's dear human life. We shall soon find what a difference it makes. Some look at a procession from a window. Others follow it on foot, have a part in it, perhaps carry an emblem. In like manner some contemplate the life of Christ with a pious but theoretical eye. We must have a part in it if it is to influence our lives.

In one of his homilies St. Bonaventure teaches us how we may visit the Child Jesus in Egypt. What he says may serve as a model for other contemplations. "Now let us dwell for a while on this homecoming of the Lord, for the consideration of these things is right profitable unto piety. Go back, therefore, unto Egypt, that thou mayest visit the Child Jesus, and when thou hast found Him, peradventure with other children out of doors, He will run to greet thee beholding thee, for He is a kindly Child, and pleasant withal to speak to. And kneeling down thou shalt kiss His feet, and taking Him up in thine arms, in silence thou shalt have joy in Him for a little space. And at last, it may be, He will say to thee—Leave hath been given us to return to our own land, and to-morrow we must depart hence: in a good hour hast thou come, for thou shalt go back in our company. And with glad promptness thou shalt make reply that great is thy joy thereat, for that thou desirest to follow Him whithersoever He fareth; and thou shalt take delight in this manner of colloquy with Him. (I said to thee just now, that it is very profitable to ponder in this sort matters that seem childish; afterwards they lead us to greater things.) And then He will conduct thee to His Mother, and honour thee with all courtesy. And for thy part thou shalt fall upon thy knees and do her reverence, honouring likewise the holy old man Joseph; and with them thou shalt abide in quiet."

Does this seem more like the contemplation of the simple Curé of Ars than of a Doctor of the Church? If so, it may help to correct our false notion that contemplation is something very deep and difficult, fit only for Carthusians and Carmelites, and beyond the reach of ordinary Christians in the world.

Hear, too, how St. Bernard, another Doctor, would have us consider the mystery of the Annunciation. "Hasten, O mothers, make haste, daughters, to the cottage of Nazareth, where the Angel is saluting Mary. Put your ear to the door to hear what he is saying; it may be you will get some word of comfort for yourselves."

Surely there is encouragement for us here. Be we as simple and as childlike as we may in our intercourse with Jesus and Mary, we shall be left behind by St. Bernard and St. Bonaventure. Notice how St. Bonaventure warns us not to neglect to "ponder matters that seem childish, for they lead to greater things." Notice too how practical is the contemplation and prayer of these two great Doctors. We are to "abide with Jesus, Mary, and Joseph in quiet:" to get "some word of comfort for ourselves."

The works and acts that reveal the hearts of Jesus and Mary lead us to reflect on our own hearts and to compare them with theirs. I say to myself—"Is that like me? Have I acted thus? I wish to do so now: help me, Lord!"

We may propose to ourselves as a general fruit "to know our Lord more clearly, that we may love Him more dearly, and follow Him more nearly," rejoicing with Him and his blessed Mother in the Joyful mysteries; sympathising with them in the Sorrowful; congratulating them in the Glorious. In all learning of them how to comport ourselves in the circumstances of our lives that resemble theirs. We may also gather fruit from the contemplation of the other holy persons we find in the various scenes from the reverence of Gabriel, the devotion of Simeon and Anna, the obedience of St. Joseph, the penitence of the good thief, the joy of Magdalen in the Resurrection, etc.

The particular fruit we ask may be determined, either by the mystery we are contemplating, which, may exhibit some virtue in stronger relief than others, or by the needs of the hour. Thus we may habitually ask for humility in the first Joyful mystery, in which we see God humbling Himself, taking the form of a servant, and Mary humbling herself as the handmaid of the Lord; for zeal, or charity to our neighbour in the mystery of the Visitation, which shows us our Lord hastening to bestow on His precursor the fruits of Redemption, and His Blessed Mother carrying out the precept, "Freely you have received, freely give." Or we may, as we have seen, go to our Lord or His Holy Mother to open our hearts to them in any pressing anxiety or trouble. A cross looms in the distance and we have to prepare ourselves. We go to the Garden of Gethsemane and to the scenes of the scourging and the crowning with thorns. We follow our Lord along the Way of the Cross, and stand with Mary on Calvary, seeking in all these mysteries for the same fruit—patience, conformity with God's Will, a trust in Him that no trial can shake. Before our eyes we have the Model of perfect suffering, and the simple, loving contemplation of Him will conform our hearts to His.

We may if we like have a different intention for each decade—*e.g.*, for the Holy Father, for a conversion, for the Holy Souls, and habitually connect our intention with one of the mysteries, Joyful, Sorrowful, or Glorious, that seems to bear most conformity with it, although in every mystery we may find a fruit corresponding with the needs of the hour. Christ descending on to the altar at the time of Holy Mass finds Himself surrounded by as many needs and troubles as there are faithful gathered together. The Church touchingly commends to Him all her needy children in the words—"And all here present whose faith and devotion are known to Thee." The one Sacrifice offered for all is different in its application to each. Each soul lays its own burden and wants before the throne of grace, and finds grace, its own needed grace, in seasonable aid. The same in its measure is true of the Rosary. No two who kneel in spirit in the chamber of the Annunciation, at the pillar of the Scourging, in the garden of the Resurrection, see the mystery under the same aspect; no two put up precisely the same prayer, or want the same grace. Our bright hours and our hopes we can sanctify by bringing them into contact with the Joyful mysteries: weighed down beneath some crushing sorrow or anxiety, we find in the Sorrowful the support and consolation we need: whilst the Glorious lend themselves admirably to thanksgiving and to that best and highest form of prayer, pure praise, in which the view of self and its needs is lost in all-absorbing delight in the greatness and goodness of God.

"Do you say your beads every day, Biddy?" an old Irishwoman was asked.

"An' is it a haythan ye'd be takin me for!" was the indignant reply. "Would I be niglictin' the Mother o' God by missin' a day? An' sure an it's twice I be sayin' it; only the first half o' the Hail Mary the second time, an' that I give her *for herself*—it's mane to be always askin', so it is."

Could we take a lesson from Biddy, any of us?

We see, then, that there are many, very many ways of saying the Rosary. They are as various as our different characters, needs, and circumstances. No way will commend itself to all, or be suitable, perhaps, for the same person at all times. What we devise for ourselves will probably help us more than anything suggested by another. We may have several methods which may be varied, interwoven, set aside, as moods and seasons succeed one another. What helps to-day may hinder to-morrow. But by a little effort and by practice we can come to be so at home in the scenes of our Lord's Life, as contemplated in the Rosary, that we turn to them naturally in every necessity, and find in them all we need.

But, it may be urged, why disturb our contemplation by mingling it with vocal prayer, which oftener than not is out of keeping with the subject? And, on the other hand, why use holy words to the sense of which we are not fully adverting? One answer is that, for the generality of us, contemplation for any length of time would be an impossibility without the sustaining force of vocal prayer. Take away the words, and the fifteen mysteries would cease to be what they are to the millions of the Church's children. Try to meditate on any one of them and you will find this to be so. The words are to the mind what the line is to the train—perfectly distinct, yet keeping it on the right track. Often, however, the words fall in with the subject of our contemplation, and suggest the fittest of terms in which the affections suggested by the mysteries may be expressed. The intention of the Church in thus uniting mental and vocal power is that one should help the other, and it is only in the case of those who are absolutely incapable of the mental part, that the Church dispenses with it as a condition of gaining the Rosary indulgences.

Nevertheless, the combination is to some a real difficulty. It is worth while, therefore, to consider how it may be met. When the words fall in naturally with the subject of the mystery they will be readily acknowledged as most helpful.

But when they do not so obviously bear upon it, are they to be strained to bring them into relation with it? Are we to try to connect each petition of the Lord's Prayer and each phrase of the Hail Mary with some point in the mystery we are considering? To most of us such an effort would be most irksome, not to say injurious. No doubt the several petitions of the Lord's Prayer will vary in significance with the mystery under consideration, and the Hail Mary have a quite different meaning in the chamber of the Annunciation, on the road to Calvary, and where the Mother and Son meet after the Resurrection. But unless the connection between the mystery and the words be more or less obvious, a search for it will not help us, and will in most cases be fatal to the ends of prayer.

We may profitably follow the advice to dwell on a word or phrase as long as it affords food for mind or heart; or we may leave the meaning of the words alone, and whilst reciting them give our minds wholly to the mystery we are contemplating. For, from the teaching of the catechism, "those do not pray well who at their prayers think neither of God nor of what they say," we learn that we may attend to the sense of the words, or, without adverting to these, occupy ourselves with God.

There are those who find a certain "irreverence in using words so holy simply as the sands of a glass for measuring time." But surely to accompany meditation on the holiest of mysteries with the holiest of words, designed to this end by the Church herself, is no mere measuring of time; rather is it giving to God the reasonable service of the whole being to which the Apostle exhorts us.

I. The Joyful Mysteries

The Annunciation

I. The Word was made flesh and dwelt amongst us.—John i.

AND in the sixth month the Angel Gabriel was sent from God into a city of Galilee, called Nazareth, to a virgin espoused to a man whoso name was Joseph, of the house of David; and the virgin's name was Mary. And the Angel, being come in, said unto her: Hail full of grace, the Lord is with thee: blessed art thou among women. Who having heard was troubled at his saying, and thought with herself what manner of salutation this should be. And the Angel said to her: Fear not, Mary, for thou hast found grace with God. Behold thou shalt conceive in thy womb, and shalt bring forth a Son. And thou shalt call His name Jesus.

He shall be great, and shall be called the Son of the Most High, and the Lord God shall give unto Him the throne of David His father: and He shall reign in the house of Jacob for ever, and of His kingdom there shall be no end. And Mary said to the Angel: How shall this be done, because I know not man? And the Angel, answering, said to her: The Holy Ghost shall come upon thee, and the power of the Most High shall overshadow thee. And therefore also the Holy which shall be born of thee, shall be called the Son of God. And behold thy cousin Elizabeth she also hath conceived a son in her old age; and this is the sixth month with her that is called barren, because no word shall be impossible with God. And Mary said: Behold the handmaid of the Lord, be it done to me according to thy word. And the Angel departed from her.—(Luke 20-38.)

See the spot—Nazareth amid the hills. At the bottom of a steep street—the little town above it—a small stone building in front of a cave, the door opening into the chamber of the Annunciation. See our Lady at prayer: the Angel entering and kneeling to salute her.

II. The Lord of all things hath loved her.—Wisd. vii.

A divine romance: the Lord of heaven and earth offering the most sublime of alliances to a girl of fourteen: sending a suitable ambassador on such a mission, one of the seven who stand before God to the chosen Mother of God.

She must have been a wonderful girl, profoundly interesting, even from a simply natural point of view. Her own words show her to have been steeped in the history and traditions of her race. Its sacred lore had been her meditation from childhood. The promises "to Abraham and to our fathers" filled her imagination and heart. And as a Jewish maiden she longed, above all private and personal blessings, for His coming who was to be the glory of Israel.

The intercourse between Mary and her Creator was free, direct, uninterrupted. No obstruction of sin or imperfection, no attachment to anything of this world impeded the flow of her affections towards Him. Through all its avenues her soul lay open to the divine influences. By day and by night there flowed into it an unbroken stream of grace. Mary knew that God had done great things for her, and she responded with perfect fidelity. Never a moment's faltering, never a thought, word, or deed that fell short of His desires. Thus, when the supreme hour of her life came, she was ready.

We read in the Scriptures how God was wont to bid His servants prepare themselves for His special favours. Moses was ordered to take off his shoes before drawing near to the burning bush, and to dispose himself by forty days' fast for converse with God on Sinai. The lips of Isaias were cleansed that they might declare divine things. Judith and Esther prepared by fasting and self-humiliation for the work to which they were called. But when the mystery of the Annunciation was to be announced to Mary, God saw there was no need of any conscious preparation on her part. He was not unmindful of what was due to Him. He knew what His infinite dignity required in the Mother He had chosen. And Mary's dispositions satisfied him. "*Quem meruisti portare*," whom thou didst deserve to bear.

Unforeseen occurrences that call upon us for immediate action reveal what we are. The Annunciation revealed Mary. There are those who refuse to accept the history on the ground that such self-possession and self-control in a child argues a height of virtue, not improbable only, but superhuman and impossible. And surely we are right in believing that none but Mary would have stood the test. Her midnight prayer interrupted by the salutation of an Archangel; the whole plan of her life reversed; a dignity without a parallel offered for her acceptance—and her mind retains its balance undisturbed. When this same Angel showed himself to Daniel, "there remained no strength in him, and he fainted away, and lay in a consternation upon his face."—(Daniel 10.) Mary is troubled indeed for a little space, but at his words, not at his appearance. She treats with him of the advent of the long-expected Messias, the Incarnation of the Son of God, the Redemption of the human race. There is no surprise, no elation, no protestation of unworthiness. Her sole thought is to ascertain the Will of God, and, when this is declared, to accept it with all it involves, because it is His Will.

O, marvellous child, mature in the difficult virtues to which saints at the end of their course scarcely attain, truly thy foundations are upon the holy mountains, where shall thy consummation be!

> III. While all things were in quiet silence and the night was in the midst of her course Thy Almighty Word leapt down from Heaven.—Wisd. xviii.

The world was in peace. All things were in quiet silence in Nazareth, in Joseph's little home, in Mary's chamber. There was a deeper stillness than usual in Mary's ever peaceful heart, for the Prince of Peace was on His way to her. Her heart was watching and praying as was its wont, pleading with a vehemence of supplication such as had never risen from earth before: "Send forth, O Lord, the Lamb, the Ruler of the earth" (Is. 16); "O that Thou wouldst rend the heavens and come down!" (Is. 64); "O God, make haste" (Ps. 70); "O God, be not slack!"(Ps. 39). Yet no sound broke on the stillness. "While all things were in quiet silence Thy Almighty Word leapt down from heaven." "Let all flesh be silent at the presence of the Lord; for He is risen up out of His holy habitation."—(Zach. 2.) And Mary bowed herself down to adore, for God had come: "the Word was made flesh and dwelt among us."—(John 1.)

All things are in quiet silence around the altar, priest and people awaiting the daily Advent. "Be silent before the face of the Lord God, for the Lord hath prepared a Victim."—(Soph. 1.) In the hush He comes as He came at Nazareth. The Word made flesh dwells among us. And like Mary, we fall down and adore.

O Prince of Peace, O Word of God, let there be quiet silence in my soul when in Holy Communion Thou comest to dwell with me. Let there be quiet in my memory and in my imagination. Let my senses be held in check, and the sights and sounds of earth be banished for the brief moments of Thy stay. Lay Thy hand upon my troubled heart, Say to its passions, its cares, its restless desires: "Peace, be still!" that in the stillness I may hear what the Lord God will speak in me.

IV. The Angel Gabriel was sent from God to a virgin espoused to a man whose name was Joseph, and the virgin's name was Mary.—Luke i.

(1) See Mary at prayer; notice her stillness, her reverence, her application.

(2) See the Angel entering; note his attitude as he says: "Hail, full of grace!"

(3) See Mary troubled, but preserving her presence of mind; not interrupting, not answering; finding out the character of the message before committing herself.

(4) Note the admirable delicacy and prudence of her questions and her answers.

(5) Observe how absolutely she effaces self, seeking one thing only—to know God's good pleasure.

(6) Watch with the eyes of faith the scene around this girl of fourteen—patriarchs, prophets, and kings, her ancestors, the saints of the ancient covenant, look upon her with paternal affection, admiration, and hope. The angelic hosts expect the "Fiat" that is to repair their ranks. The Eternal Trinity awaits her consent, to carry into effect the decree for the redemption of man.

(7) Hear the worship, self-abasement, obedience, thankfulness, abandonment to God, in her "*Ecce ancilla Domini.*"

(8) Adore with Gabriel, with the whole angelic host, with all saints of the Old and New Covenants the Word made flesh.

(9) Rejoice at the infinite glory God begins to receive from One of our race.

(10) Invite Him who came to Mary to come to you in Holy Communion. "Come, Lord Jesus!"

V. **The Most High hath sanctified his own tabernacle.**—Ps. xlv.

> But fourteen years and full of grace,
> A shrine so fair,
> That God must needs content Himself
> By dwelling there.
>
> O wondrous child, sole confidant
> Of the Most High,
> Sole arbiter with Him, of our
> Dread destiny,

> Speak! mid creation's silence be
> Thy "Fiat" heard;
> Its swift response, thy God Himself,
> The Eternal Word.

VI. My heart delighted in her.—Ecclus. li.

(1) Thou art all fair, O my love, and there is not a spot in thee (Cant. 4).

(2) Thou wast perfect in thy ways from the day of thy creation (Ezechiel 28).

One is My dove, My perfect one is but one (Cant. 6).

(3) Hearken, daughter, and see and incline thy ear…and the King shall greatly desire thy beauty, for He is the Lord thy God (Ps. 44).

(4) Behold the joy that cometh to thee from God! (Baruch 4).

(5) Behold the Lord God shall come! (Isaias 40).

(6) Thine eyes shall see the King in His beauty (Isaias 33).

(7) My soul doth magnify the Lord, and my spirit hath rejoiced in God my Saviour. Because he hath regarded the humility of His handmaid; for behold from henceforth all generations shall call me blessed. Because He that is mighty hath done great things to me, and holy is His name (Luke 1).

(8) Joy is come upon me from the Holy One (Baruch 4).

(9) I will be glad and rejoice in Thee: I will sing to thy name, O Thou Most High (Ps. 9).

(10) I will rejoice in the Lord: and I will joy in God my Jesus (Habacuc 3).

The Visitation

I. Whithersoever she entereth God will give a blessing.—Ecclus. iv.

AND Mary rising up in those days, went into the hill country with haste into a city of Juda. And she entered into the house of Zachary, and saluted Elizabeth. And it came to pass that when Elizabeth heard the salutation of Mary, the infant leaped in her womb. And Elizabeth was filled with the Holy Ghost. And she cried out with a loud voice, and said—Blessed art thou among women, and blessed is the fruit of thy womb. And whence is this to me, that the mother of my Lord should come to me? For behold as soon as the voice of thy salutation sounded in my ears, the infant in my womb leaped for joy. And blessed art thou that hast believed, because those things shall be accomplished that were spoken to thee by the Lord. And Mary said—My soul doth magnify the Lord: and my spirit hath rejoiced in God my Saviour (Luke 1).

See the hilly road from Nazareth to Hebron. The house of Zachary and Elizabeth. Our Lady on her journey, and at the moment she greets Elizabeth. See the aged saint sinking on her knees before the Mother of her Lord. Hear the sweet tones of the *Magnificat*.

II. Mary went with haste into the hill country.—Luke i.

Many reasons might have exempted Our Lady from this visit of charity. Many difficulties stood in the way. But faithful to every impulse of grace, she never took difficulties into account when there was question of accomplishing the Will of God. However uphill her journey through life—and it was uphill from Bethlehem to Calvary—she went forward with a simplicity and strength of purpose that never faltered. Do I go with haste into hilly country when duty or charity calls me thither?

God is never outdone in generosity. He rewards abundantly even here those who prefer His service to their own satisfaction, or rather, who make His Will their own. What consolations He had here for Mary and for those dear to her. If I try to forget myself for His sake, I shall find him going out of His way to prepare for me sweet surprises. Let me trust Him. Let me taste and see that the Lord is sweet.

What compensation for the fatigues of the journey must the Blessed Mother have found in the presence of her Son. If my road like hers lies uphill, why do I not find strength and comfort in Jesus, present with me always by sanctifying grace, and present Body and Blood and Soul and Divinity as often as I desire—as really present as He was with Mary!

Had I been in her company and so near to Christ, should I have found the road over rugged and tedious? How is it that my quarter-of-an-hour's thanksgiving after Communion seems so long? Mother of God, get me something of thy faith and thy love. Holy Mary, Mother of God, pray for us sinners *now*.

If the saints have revealed Christ in the whole tenour of their lives, so as to be "other Christs," how must He have shone forth in Mary, and worked through her means during her stay with Elizabeth. Oh that in virtue of my Communions He would live and work in me! That he would make me kind in my thoughts, in my words, in my looks, in my listening, in the tone of my voice, in my offers of help, in my visits, in my interpretations; that I could live by Him, speak by Him, work through Him, be in my little measure His instrument as Mary was! Holy Mary, Mother of God, pray for us sinners *now*.

> III. Her conversation hath no bitterness, nor her company any tediousness, but joy and gladness.—Wisd. viii.

Consider the conversation of the two holy cousins. How interesting, edifying, profitable, it was. Interesting, as dealing with the most momentous question of that age and of every age—the fulfilment of the promises of God, the coming of His Son upon the earth for the redemption of all nations. Edifying and profitable, because not occupied with trivialities—mere chit-chat, the retailing of news, the shortcomings of others—like so many conversations of even good people, but elevating and helpful, promoting directly or indirectly the glory of God.

It was not all on the lines of the *Magnificat*: there were tender greetings interchanged and words of affectionate solicitude. But with God so near, in what direction must their thoughts and their words have been ever tending? Where could their hearts be but with their treasure?

What is my conversation like? Presuming it to be harmless, is this its only merit? When the topics of the hour or of daily life are discussed after the ordinary fashion, do I ever strike a higher note, or by a word of sympathy or encouragement draw forth the riches hidden in the heart of another?

Mary's heart was full, but it needed the loving congratulations of her cousin to unlock its treasures and give the *Magnificat* to the world.

I will ask our Lady to watch over and to bless my intercourse with others. Holy Mary, Mother of God, pray for us sinners *now*.

IV. In her is the spirit of understanding, holy, active, sweet.—Wisd. vii.

See our Lady on her journey to Hebron—leaving her poor home in Galilee, a despised province, whose people were uncouth and of ill-repute—and making her way to Judea, the home of all the culture Palestine possessed, where were the Temple and the schools of the learned. Zachary and Elizabeth, if not wealthy, were in easy circumstances, persons of consideration, not in their own little town only, but in the Holy City, when the Temple services took them thither. Mary, a poor girl from the country, advanced timidly, ignorant of God's designs in this visit, thinking only of carrying out the inspiration He had given her.

Let us look at her in these last days of her girlhood, before the responsibilities and anxieties of motherhood have begun.

Nothing that comes from the hand of God is so beautiful as the soul of a child. What must this child have been, whose face reflected the innocence of her soul and the beauty of her character, whose every word and movement by its charm and grace gave her an attractiveness unsurpassed till then, and only to be surpassed by the attractiveness of her Child who was God! To look on her would have made our hearts beat high.

(1) Notice how the immediate effect of God's presence is to enkindle zeal for souls.

(2) The sanctification of the Precursor was attached by God to Mary's salutation. To this end He inspired her to visit her cousin. How much depends on fidelity to the whisperings of grace!

(3) Fidelity brooks no delay. Mary went in haste.

(4) In haste, not in hurry. The God of peace entrusts His work to peaceful souls. "The Lord is not in a whirlwind" (3 Kings 19).

(5) Mary salutes Elizabeth. The higher in dignity is the readier with the graceful acts of courtesy that charity inspires. Do I stand upon my dignity overmuch, to the detriment of charity?

(6) What trivial acts God uses for His purposes! Mary's affectionate greeting was the channel of grace to the Baptist!

(7) With the instinct of humility Mary hides her secret even from such a kindred spirit as Elizabeth's.

(8) But finding that God had revealed it for the consolation of both, she refers all praise to Him with the instinct of love.

(9) In the *Magnificat* she pours forth her soul in the most glorious act of praise earth had ever heard.

(10) And then she descends to little, lowly, household duties—handmaid, not of the Lord only but of Elizabeth,

servant of a servant of God. Am I in any degree like her?

℣. Freely have you received, freely give.—Matthew x.

> Hasten o'er the mountains,
> Unto Hebron be
> Bearer of the Blessing
> Gabriel brought to thee:
>
> Sing thy song of gladness
> For a world restored,
> Mouthpiece of creation,
> Magnify the Lord!

VI. Charity is kind—I Cor. xiii.

(1) Let us love one another, for charity is of God (1 John 4).

(2) Let us not love in word nor in tongue, but in deed and in truth (1 John 3).

(3) Loving one another with the charity of brotherhood, with honour preventing one another…communicating to the necessities of the saints (Rom. 12).

(4) Rejoice with them that rejoice, weep with them that weep. Not minding high things, but consenting to the humble (Rom. 12).

(5) Freely have you received, freely give (Matth. 10).

(6) According to thy ability be merciful. If thou have much give abundantly (Tobias 4).

(7) He gave to every one of them commandment concerning his neighbour (Ecclus 17).

(8) Every one shall help his neighbour, and shall say to his brother: Be of good courage (Isaias 41).

(9) Hast thou heard a word against thy neighbour, let it die within thee. And believe not every word. There is one that

slippeth with the tongue, but not from the heart. For who is there that hath not offended with the tongue? (Ecclus. 19).

(10) God gave to Solomon wisdom and understanding exceeding much, and largeness of heart as the sand that is on the seashore (III. Kings 4).

The Nativity

I. This is God, our God, unto eternity, and for ever and ever.—Ps. xlvii.

AND it came to pass that in those days there went out a decree from Caesar Augustus, that the whole world should be enrolled. This enrolling was first made by Cyrinus the governor of Syria. And all went to be enrolled, every one into his own city. And Joseph also went up from Galilee out of the city of Nazareth into Judea, to the city of David, which is called Bethlehem, because he was of the house and family of David, to be enrolled with Mary his espoused wife, who was with child. And it came to pass, that when they were there, her days were accomplished, that she should be delivered. And she brought forth her first-born

Son, and wrapped Him up in swaddling clothes, and laid Him in a manger, because there was no room for Him in the inn. And there were in the same country shepherds watching, and keeping the night watches over their flocks. And behold an Angel of the Lord stood by them, and the brightness of God shone round about them, and they feared with a great fear. And the Angel said unto them: Fear not: for behold I bring you good tidings of great joy, that shall be in all the people; for this day is born to you a Saviour, who is Christ the Lord, in the city of David. And this shall be a sign unto you: you shall find the Infant wrapped in swaddling clothes, and laid in a manger. And suddenly there was with the Angel a multitude of the heavenly army, praising God and saying: Glory to God in the highest: and on earth peace to men of good-will. And it came to pass after the Angels departed from them into heaven, the shepherds said to one another: Let us go over to Bethlehem, and let us see this word that is come to pass which the Lord hath shewed to us. And they came with haste; and they found Mary and Joseph, and the Infant lying in the manger. And seeing, they understood the word that had been spoken to them concerning this Child. And all that heard wondered: and at those things that were told them by the shepherds. But Mary kept all these words, pondering them in her heart. And the shepherds returned, glorifying and praising God, for all the things they had heard and seen, as it was told unto them (Luke 2).

See the cave stable, dark, cold, bare. See the moisture trickling down the walls. Feel the bleak wind of the December night as it rushes up the slope and sweeps in, searching its every nook. See where on one side of the unprotected place, the manger stands. On a few handfuls of straw, such as might be found in a wayside, neglected stable, the Infant lies.

 II. How hath He not with Him given us all things?—Romans viii

He lays Himself down on the straw in the coldest hour of the winter's night. His little limbs are trembling, and there are tears of pain in His eyes. But He stretches out His arms to us, and the smile on His lips says:

Here I am. I am come at last. Take Me and do with Me what you will. I am come to be your little servant, to be of use to you in any way that I can.

You need a Redeemer: I will redeem you when I am old enough. I am too small to be crucified yet, but when I am grown up I will shed the last drop of My blood for you. In a week's time I will give some to show you I am ready to give all.

You need a physician, for you are sick. I have medicine for every pain and disease; I will cure you.

You need a master. I will teach you with My words as soon as I can speak, and meantime if you come to My crib, come up close enough, look long enough, you will learn many things from Me even now.

You need a companion and a friend. That is just what I have come for—to be a companion that will never leave your side, a friend who will love you dearly, never tire of you, never weary of listening to your troubles, always be thinking of you; who will watch over you, share your joys and your sorrows; advise, warn, encourage you, provide for you in every need.

You want food. Even this I will be to you. I will come into your heart to give you strength to work out your salvation grandly; to make you grow up like Me; to make it easy and pleasant to do even hard things, things that cost, things that hurt.

You want a brother. I have come all the way from heaven to be your Brother. I have taken your nature that I may be like you in all things. Look at Me and see. I have hands, and feet, and eyes, and heart like you, that I may feel as you feel, bear pain as you have to bear it, work as you must do, and be an example to you in working and in suffering. I am your Brother, come to take you by the hand and lead you to My Father, who will love you for My sake.

Yes, I am all yours, do with Me what you like. Will you find it in your heart to hurt Me? I know you will. I know what your sins will cost me. I know what is going to happen to My hands, and feet, and side. But I am ready for it all, if only you will let me save you, and take you back with Me to heaven. Do not turn from Me; do not disappoint Me. Listen to Me; follow Me; return Me love for love.

III. There was no room in the inn.—Luke ii.

Bethlehem did not rise up and thrust Him out of its precincts as Nazareth did later. He had to seek outside for such shelter as a stable could give, simply because there was no room for Him in the little place. It was crowded up with other things. Is my heart a Bethlehem?

Bethlehem was His own city. Yet there was no room. "He came unto His own, and His own received Him not." I am His own, and He comes to me. "Behold I stand at the door and knock." Do I rise and open to Him? Or do I say from behind the closed door: "There is no room"?

Some creature, some passion, some sin, perhaps, disputes my heart with Thee, Lord! There is no room.

Thou cravest a larger space in my life, in my day a Communion at less distant intervals, a few minutes taken from pleasure or from trifles to visit Thy neglected tabernacle in the neighbouring church. But it would not be convenient, it would interfere with my arrangements. There is no room.

How long, Lord, how long! Remember that whilst thou waitest our consent, and wilt offer no violence to our free will, Thou art still God, and all power is given to Thee in heaven and in earth.

Make room for Thyself within my heart, O Lord! Say in the tone of authority of days gone by: "Take these things hence" (John 2). "Take the stumbling-blocks out of my way" (Isaias 57). "The place is too straight for Me, make Me room to dwell in." (*Ibid* 49).

And I will make answer: "My heart is ready, God, my heart is ready" (Ps. 107).

IV. And the shepherds said one to another: Let us go over to Bethlehem, and let us see this word that is come to pass.—Luke ii.

One reason why we scarcely penetrate beneath the surface of the mysteries of our Lord's life, is the dullness of our desires. Were we eager like the shepherds, and faithful to the leadings of grace, we should come to understand as they did. Let us go over to Bethlehem and see this word that is come to pass…And they came in haste…*And seeing, they understood.* We should understand better if, like Daniel, we were men of desires, if we took some trouble to concentrate our thoughts on the truths our faith presents to us. No one ever pondered mysteries like Mary, who saw further at a glance than others have seen in a lifetime of contemplation. Her magnificent mind gave itself with out distraction or interruption to the study of her Babe, and lost in His greatness, cried out unceasingly: "Who is able to declare His works? Who shall show forth the power of His majesty, or who shall be able to declare His mercy?...Neither is it possible to find out the glorious works of God. When a man hath done then shall he begin" (Ecclus. 18).

> V. She brought forth her first-born Son, and wrapped Him up in swaddling clothes, and laid Him in a manger.—Luke ii.

To whom does He trust Himself in His helpless infancy? To Mary. There is a lesson for us here. It was an apparent waste of time to spend so many years in Mary's arms, on Mary's knee, when, had He come into the world as Adam did, He might have been teaching from the moment He began to dwell amongst us. But He was teaching by His actions from the first. We too must be nursed and cared for by Mary. Our Christian life must develop under her protection. We must run to her, cling to her, trust to her guidance. The first condition of following Jesus is to be a child of Mary. I will ask her to care for me as she cared for Him, to value and to love me for His sake.

> VI. My thoughts are not your thoughts, nor your ways My ways.—Isaias lv.

(1) In that tiny frame dwells the fulness of man's intelligence and the full strength of man's will. He knows and deliberately chooses all that He finds around him at His birth.

(2) In heaven "thousands of thousands ministered to Him, and ten thousand times a hundred thousand stood before Him" (Dan. 7).

(3) On earth he is treated like the very beasts. A cold damp shed is shelter good enough for Mary's tender Babe. But earth's provision for Him is also His own free choice.

(4) Why? His body, exquisitely fashioned, is sensitive as no other child's could be to the hardships of His lot. Why is that lot so hard? Why does He deliberately seek out and draw to Himself such want and pain, when a single tear or prayer would have redeemed us?

(5) Because Divine Wisdom takes, not the easiest and pleasantest, but the surest, means of attaining Its end. How could our Master have taught us better the lessons He came to teach! He knows what is due to His Majesty, yet He bespeaks what to our seeming is so unworthy of Him, because it is not our redemption only that He has come to secure, but our hearts. If with all He has done for me I have so little love for Him; if with the sight of Him before me, suffering from the moment of His birth, I find it so hard to bear the least pain or inconvenience, what should I have been without the spur of His example? Poor little Infant Jesus! He knew that He could not do too much, He could not begin to suffer too early to win the love of some of us. Has He won my love yet?

(6) Bethlehem is the reversal of the world's judgments respecting honours, riches, convenience, comforts.

(7) Bethlehem is the revelation of God's thoughts in regard to poverty, privation, oblivion, pain.

(8) Bethlehem is a startling indication of the way in which He is going to redeem the world and lead us back to the heaven selfishness had lost.

O Babe of Bethlehem, rectify my thoughts and my ways by Thine!

VII. Who is this?—Isaias lxiii.

Let us kneel by the young Mother and see what she saw that first Christmas night.

(1) She saw lying on straw a weak and trembling child. And she adored Him as the Lord of heaven and earth, who established the mountains, and holds the waters in the hollow of His hand.

(2) She saw His frail beauty, and knew Him to be the most mighty God. "I am, I am the Lord, and there is no Saviour besides Me"(Isaias 43).

(3) He was but an hour old, and she worshipped Him as the Ancient of Days, begotten before the eternal years.

(4) He was her Babe. He belonged to her as no child ever belonged to its mother. Yet she was His creature and depended on Him absolutely. All her graces were the gift of those tiny hands; all were purchased by the blood that flowed through those delicate veins and vivified that Heart.

(5) "I am the Lord, I am the Lord." This was the truth ever present, ever new to her. She was lost in astonishment that the Most High should be so lowly, that One so mighty should be so sweet. She bowed herself down to adore Him. She took Him into her arms and pressed her trembling lips against His brow.

(6) When the coldness of our hearts chills even ourselves, what a resource we have in Mary's worship and in Mary's praise!

(7) What a consolation that she represented us in Bethlehem; that we may appropriate and offer to the Infant Jesus the treasures of His Mother's heart.

(8) Share with us, Mother of God, thy faith and wonder, and delight beside the manger. Win and warm our hearts

by the attractiveness of thy Babe. "The Lord is great and exceedingly to be praised: the Lord is little and exceedingly to be loved."

VIII. Mary kept all these words, pondering them in her heart.—Luke ii.

> O blessed eyes that saw Him come at last,
>   The Promised One,
> O happy arms that held enfolded fast
>   The Eternal Son:
>
> O heart that stored the memories of that night
>   So sweet and stern,
> Teach me to ponder Bethlehem aright,
>   To look and learn!

IX. Fear not: Behold your God.—Isaias xl.

(1) Lo, this is our God; we have waited for Him and He will save us…we have patiently waited for Him; we shall rejoice and be joyful in His salvation (Isaias 35).

(2) This is God, our God, unto eternity and for ever and ever (Ps. 47).

(3) In Him dwelleth all the fulness of the Godhead corporally (Col. 2).

(4) O God, how great are Thy works, Thy thoughts are exceeding deep (Ps. 91).

(5) Truly Thou art a hidden God, the God of Israel, the Saviour (Isaias 45).

(6) Thou alone art my King and my God (Ps. 40).

(7) The eternal King of worlds (Tobias 13).

(8) Come and reign over us (Judges 9).

(9) Come and teach us what we ought to do (Judges 13).

The Presentation

I. Blessed art Thou in the holy Temple of Thy glory.—Daniel iii.

AND after the days of the purification of Mary, according to the law of Moses, were accomplished, they carried Jesus to Jerusalem, to present Him to the Lord, as it is written in the law of the Lord: *Every male opening the womb shall be called holy to the Lord*; and to offer a sacrifice according as it is written in the law of the Lord, a pair of turtle doves, or two young pigeons. And behold there was a man in Jerusalem named Simeon, and this man was just and devout, waiting for the consolation of Israel; and the Holy Ghost was in him. And he had received an answer from the Holy Ghost, that he should not see death, before he had seen the Christ of the Lord. And he came by the Spirit into the Temple. And when His parents brought in the Child Jesus, to do for Him according to the custom of the law, he also took Him in his arms, and blessed God, and said: Now Thou dost dismiss Thy servant, Lord, according to Thy word, in peace: because my eyes have seen Thy salvation, which Thou hast prepared before the face of all peoples; a light to the revelation of the Gentiles, and the glory of Thy people Israel.

And His father and mother were wondering at those things which were spoken concerning Him. And Simeon blessed them and said to Mary His Mother: Behold this Child is set for the fall and for the resurrection of many in Israel, and for a sign which shall be contradicted; and thy own soul a sword shall pierce, that out of many hearts thoughts may be revealed. And there was one Anna, a prophetess, the daughter of Phanuel, of the tribe of Aser; she was far advanced in years, and had lived with her husband seven years from her virginity; and she was a widow until fourscore and four years; who departed not from the Temple, by fastings and prayers serving night and day. Now she at the same hour coming in, confessed to the Lord, and spoke of Him to all that looked for the redemption of Israel (Luke 2).

See the Jewish mothers making their way up the Temple steps, their babes in their arms. Hear the bleating of the lambs, the cooing of the doves. See the blessed Mother and her divine Child: St. Joseph by her side; in his hand the wicker cage with the doves, and five shekels (about fifteen shillings of our money) for the redemption of the Child. Look at the face of Mary at the moment she offers her Son to God.

See Mary and Joseph and the prophetess Anna gathered round holy Simeon who holds in his arms the Christ of the Lord.

II. Bless the Lord all ye servants of the Lord, who stand in the house of the Lord, in the courts of the house of our God.—Ps. cxxxiii.

Let me learn a lesson from each one in this blessed group.

(1) The Divine Child.

The greatest, of all, the Creator and Lord of all, is small, weak, silent, dependent. Scripture ridicules the impotent gods of the heathen: to what a state of helplessness has love reduced the true God here! Is there anything in that little face to reveal to us the treasures of His Heart—Its vast design for the glory of His Father and the salvation of men; Its steadfastness of purpose that neither suffering nor ingratitude will overcome; Its generosity that only Calvary and the perpetual immolation of the Eucharist will satisfy? It is the need of giving Himself unreservedly to those whom He loves that brings Him to the Temple to-day: "Sacrifice and oblation Thou wouldst not, then said I, Behold I Come" (Ps. 39). He offers Himself to a life of hardship and persecution, to a death of agony and shame. And makes His offering with the eagerness of love that counts no cost: "He hath rejoiced as a giant to run His way" (Ps. 18). Sacrifice is the necessity of love, its instinct, its language, its food, its very life. O little Babe, do I recognise by this mark my love of Thee?

(2) The Blessed Mother.

Mary gave a gift to God such as had never before been offered to Him, greater than which no man can give. And

God gave her in return the assurance of a lifelong sorrow. His reward seems strange to us. Yet were not trial and pain gifts worthy of God, could He have chosen such a moment for sending them to His well-beloved daughter! If His Heart went out to the widow who cast her two mites into the treasury, because she had "cast in all she had, even her whole living," how would He prize the generosity of Mary, who in offering her Son gave what was more to her than life. Those who know Him understand His ways. Mary was not disturbed. The sudden change in her life touched neither her peace nor her trust, but the perfection of her submission did not deaden her pain. The sword made its way down to the depths of her soul, to remain there till it was drawn forth on Easter Day by the same hand that had plunged it therein; drawn forth to make way for the floods of joy that filled it to overflowing. How God loves to outdo in generosity! Who has ever regretted in the end having given Him a gift that cost!

See Mary in her sorrow, not downcast, not self-concentrated; ready as before to enter into and soothe the trifling troubles of others. God could not trust me in my youth with the knowledge of the heaviest cross that would befall me. I should be soured, if not crushed. But Mary He could trust. She Left the Temple knowing what was in store for her and her Divine Son. And Joseph found her no different in her home life, unless it were that she seemed sweeter than ever, tenderer even than before with those in sorrow, because of the fellow-feeling that came to her from the pressure of her own cross.

See her taking the road home; her Child pressed close to her heart. She is to tend and rear Him as a lamb for sacrifice; to watch Him grow up in His loveliness; and in the fulness of

His beauty to give Him up to torture and to death. And this for me. Mother of God, blessed art thou among women, and blessed is the fruit of thy womb, Jesus.

> To measure love we reckon up
>   Its sacrificed:
> Who, then, shall gauge the charity
>   That offered—Christ!
>
> That gave Him to a hunted life,
>   A death of shame,
> To win, alas! from many a heart
>   Love but in name.

(3) THE FOSTER-FATHER.

St. Joseph heard the words of Simeon. How tenderly he must have sympathised with Mary. How do I behave towards those on whom a sudden sorrow has fallen?

(4) SIMEON.

Simeon's desires won for him the promise that he should not die till he had seen the Christ of the Lord. An eager heart such as his is very pleasing to God. The longing to see our Lord, to know Him intimately, to love Him dearly, is met by the answer: "Thine eyes shall see the King in His beauty" (Isaias 33).

"O Daniel, I am come to thee because thou art a man of desires," said Gabriel. And again: "Fear not, man of desires, take courage and be strong" (Dan 10).

Simeon waited patiently day after day, perhaps for many years. There was nothing to show he was nearing the realisation of his hopes. No Angel came on the morning of the Presentation to announce the happiness that was at hand. What if that day he had failed to be where duty called him! What if on the morrow he had lain dying, and, complaining to God of the non-fulfilment of the promise for which he had lived, had heard the answer: "The hour of the morning sacrifice yesterday was My hour; My Christ awaited you in the Temple, but you were not watching."

I too have desires of higher things for myself and for others. I too hope and pray through long years, relying on the promise: "Ask and you shall receive" (Matth. 7). "Know ye that no one hath hoped in the Lord and hath been confounded" (Ecclus 2). But I must do my part, not only by desires and by prayer, but by faithful service like the old man Simeon.

What did Simeon feel as he held in his arms and pressed to his heart "the Christ of the Lord"? When his eyes saw, dimly through their tears, "the Light of the Gentiles and the glory of Israel"? The same Christ I hold and embrace after Holy Communion. And if my eyes do not yet behold Him, I have the assurance: "Blessed are they who have not seen and have believed." "Thine eyes shall see the King in His beauty." Shall not this faith and this hope enkindle something of Simeon's love? If still my heart is cold, let me offer to Him who accepts desires as deeds, the love of the old man's heart that day.

(5) ANNA.

Anna was a dweller in the Temple, known and revered by all who frequented it, so constant was her attendance, so reverent her worship, so fervent her speech when she spoke of the Expectation of Israel. Yet what was there to draw her to the Temple Courts? Had every day seen a Presentation of Christ, as our daily Mass, her assiduity would have been explicable, would have been called for. Is my attendance in church assiduous, is my worship reverent? Every morning Christ is there presented to the Father: is not my presence and my homage called for?

Anna had no promise. But God is better than His word, as we shall find out in heaven. He loves to take us by surprise. He loves to answer even the unspoken desires of the heart. He delights to fill our cup of joy to the brim. It is not likely that such a dweller in the Temple would be unknown to a kindred spirit like Simeon's. Perhaps she knew of the promise to him and trusted to have a share in his joy, and therefore departed not from the Temple, by fasting and prayer serving day and night. She was near at the moment of the Presentation, as if she kept the old man in sight, to be at hand when his hour should come, ready to receive the overflowing of his grace should God vouchsafe it to her. How could God refuse to satisfy that longing for Himself which is such perfect homage, and of which, alas, He finds so little!

Anna spoke of the Child to all who looked for the redemption of Israel. Out of the abundance of the heart the mouth speaks. Because her heart was full of Him she could not but speak of Him. Do I want to know of what my heart is full? Of what do I love to speak?

> III. Now Thou dost dismiss Thy servant, O Lord,
> according to Thy word in peace.—Luke ii.

The special fruit of the Viaticum is peace. Our Lord comes to soothe and strengthen His failing servant; to befriend him when all other friends fail; to pass with him through the dark valley of the shadow of death. He Himself is the promised salvation, dear pledge in the Host of the near presence, the unveiled Face, the familiar intercourse that is at hand. How should not Thy servants, Lord Jesus, clasping Thee, held fast by Thee amid the perils of death, depart this life in peace!

> IV. And on the fortieth day they carried Him to the Temple to present Him to the Lord.—Luke ii.

(1) Look into Mary's immaculate heart and see the joy with which she presents to God the one offering worthy of Him which that magnificent Temple had seen.

(2) See St. Joseph standing by; understanding the significance of that Presentation; uniting his sacrifice with the oblation of Jesus and Mary; studying and imitating their obedience, their generosity, their sinking of self.

(3) See holy Simeon coming in as was his wont; coming in quietly for an ordinary visit, little thinking that the desire of his life is to be satisfied this day.

(4) Watch Our Lady as full of joy she places her Divine Child in the arms of the old man, not suspecting the sword of sorrow he is to give her in return.

(5) Notice the different graces God has in store for two of His favourites—a joyful surprise for one, an unexpected trial for the other, and the trial is for his best-beloved.

(6) Note, too, how God's promises are often conditional, dependent on fidelity. Simeon had received an answer from the Holy Ghost that he should not see death before he had seen the Christ of the Lord. But he had to watch, and to follow the leadings of grace, for he knew neither the day nor the hour when his Lord would come. "And he was led by the Spirit into the Temple." Had he been unfaithful that morning, he would have missed his grace. Who knows what I may miss if through mere laziness I stay away from daily

Mass! That conversion, that favour I have prayed for so long, may be in store for me in some week-day mass.

(7) Look at Simeon holding the Divine Child in that embrace which was his First and last Communion. Admire the fruits of that Communion as seen in his canticle:

Humility—"Thy servant."
Hope and trust—"Dismiss in peace."
Faith—"My eyes have seen Thy salvation."
Love—"He took Him into his arms and blessed God."

(8) "May my soul die the death of the just," the death of holy Simeon, whose life was lived for the sight of Jesus.

(9) "And my last end," my last Communion, "be like unto his."

V. He had received an answer from the Holy Ghost that he should not see death before he had seen the Christ of the Lord.—Luke ii.

(1) I will look for Thy Salvation, O Lord (Gen. 49).

Who will grant that my request may come and that God may give me what I look for? (Job 6).

(2) Hear my prayer, Lord, and my supplication, give ear to my tears (Ps. 38).

(3) The Lord is my portion…therefore will I wait for Him (Lament. 3).

(4) Expect the Lord, do manfully, and let thy heart take courage, and wait thou for the Lord (Ps. 26).

(5) Delight in the Lord, and he will give thee the requests of thy heart (Ps. 36).

(6) The Lord waiteth that He may have mercy on thee… blessed are all they that wait for Him (Isaias 30).

Thou shalt know that I am the Lord, for they shall not be confounded that wait for Me (Isaias 49).

(7) I am sent to thee, thou man of desires (Dan. 10).

(8) With expectation I have waited for the Lord, and He was attentive to me (Ps. 39).

(9) Art thou not the Lord our God whom we have looked for? (Jerem. 14).

(10) The Lord is good to them that hope in Him, to the soul that seeketh Him. It is good to wait with silence for the salvation of God (Lament. 3).

The Finding in the Temple

> I. I found Him whom my soul loveth:
> I held Him and I will not let Him go.—Cant. iii.

AND His parents went every year to Jerusalem at the solemn day of the Pasch. And when He was twelve years old, they going up into Jerusalem according to the custom of the feast, and having fulfilled the days, when they returned, the Child Jesus remained in Jerusalem, and His parents knew it not. And thinking that He was in the company, they came a day's journey, and sought Him among their kinsfolk and acquaintance. And, not finding Him, they returned into Jerusalem seeking Him.

And it came to pass that after three days they found Him in the Temple, sitting in the midst of the doctors, hearing them and asking them questions. And all that heard Him were astonished at His wisdom and His answers. And seeing Him they wondered. And His Mother said to Him: Son, why hast Thou done so to us? behold Thy father and I have sought Thee sorrowing. And He said to them: How is it that you sought Me? Did you not know that I must be about My Father's business? And they understood not the word that He spoke unto them.

And He went down with them, and came to Nazareth, and was subject to them. And His Mother kept all these words in her heart.—Luke 2.

1. See the Galilee caravan, numbering many thousands, on its way home, after its first night's halt at Beeroth. Two pilgrims have separated themselves from it, and with sad yet peaceful faces are on their way back to Jerusalem.

2. See how, footsore and weary, they thread the narrow streets of the Holy City, scanning every party that they pass, making inquiries, suffering sorely, yet considerate for others, and at peace.

3. See them on the third day entering the Temple; making their way to a hall in the Court of the Women; coming upon a group of doctors; hearing a child's voice; pressing forward; seeing the Child Jesus; meeting His eye and His smile.

> II. In the streets and the broad ways I will seek Him whom my soul loveth; I sought Him and found Him not.—Cant. iii.

Where did Mary find her Divine Child? In the Temple. The first time she sought Him there? Assuredly not. She knew too well where His Heart was likely to lead Him, not to have gone straight to the Temple, when, with weary feet and anxious hearts, she and Joseph returned to Jerusalem seeking

Him. Where should He be but in His Father's house: Not once only, but again and again during that dreary time of desolation she sought Him there. And there she found Him when the days of anguish were over. And there she had the embrace and the smile that made up to her for all her pain.

We turn instinctively to the Tabernacle in times of inward trial. And we do well. Where should we go in our trouble but to the God of all consolation? But if He does not show Himself to us as such, if the answer to prayer does not make haste to come, we lose heart, and leave off praying. We tire so soon. Our desires are so faint that almost at the outset we are ready to give over our search, and sit down and bemoan ourselves. Not so did Mary and Joseph. None ever sought Christ in the midst of such darkness and desolation as did those two faithful hearts. And none ever sought with greater diligence. Whatever place in the Holy City offered the smallest chance of finding Him, there they might be seen; going over the same ground a score of times; putting their question again and again; battling against the anguish and sinking of heart that grew with each hour of disappointment; bearing their trouble bravely; resigned to God's Will, but suffering none the less for the perfection of their endurance.

It was to serve us as an example that Mary and Joseph sought wearily for Christ. We learn from ancient records that our Lord's Apostles and first followers were wont to speak of Him amongst themselves as "our Teacher." As a good teacher He has so planned His life and actions as to be able to offer Himself to us as a model in what is hardest and most painful in our way to heaven. Where He cannot Himself be our example, He gives us as His substitute the most apt of His disciples. So we have Mary and Joseph showing us with what patience and perseverance we must seek Christ when we have lost the joy of His sensible presence. How we must search everyplace where we are likely to find Him; examine our various duties and amusements to see if anything in them is keeping Him from us; go often to the church to seek Him there, and to gain there the courage to persist in our search until we find.

III. Show me Thy face.—Cant. ii.

I compassionate thee, blessed Mother, in thy desolation. Help me in my days of darkness and discouragement. The anguish of those three days did not disturb thy peace of soul, thy confidence in God, thy resignation to His Will. Get me the grace to be drawn closer to Him by trial. Thy loss of Christ was without the smallest fault on thy part. Let me never lose Him by mortal sin. And let me hate all deliberate venial sin and negligence that builds up a barrier between my soul and Him.

Sometimes I forfeit the sense of His nearness and the freedom and happiness of my intercourse with Him by carelessness in my service of Him, in my daily duties, or by infidelity to grace. Sometimes I am left in darkness on account of sins in the past unatoned for. At times our Lord hides Himself, as He hid from His dear Magdalen, that He may see how I act when He does not seem to be by. Or He wants me to feel how poor and needy I am when left to myself. A time of trouble is often the harbinger of a great grace. It is always a sign of God's love, sent to purify and strengthen my soul, to shorten my purgatory, to earn for me a higher place in heaven. This thought will help me to bear it as Mary and Joseph bore the pain of the three days' loss, in peace, in patient trust, in the firm faith that all things, all things, without exception, work together unto good for those who love God.

IV. Son, why hast Thou done so to us?—Luke ii.

1. Mary, His Mother and confidant, whose heart beat in perfect unison with His, was kept in ignorance of His designs. Can I wonder if God's ways are often mysterious to me?

2. Because uncertainty and suspense are painful, we think that God should exempt us from them, or bring them quickly to an end. Mary felt both in this mystery, and with an intensity far beyond any suffering of ours.

3. God could have spared her this trial but did not. If "those whom He foreknew, who according to His purpose are called to be saints, must be made conformable to the image of His Son," the Man of Sorrows, how much more must the Mother of that Son be conformed to Him?

4. Her tender pleading: "Why hast Thou done so to us?" is like His cry on the Cross: "My God, My God, why hast Thou forsaken Me?"

5. And as "we have not a high-priest who cannot have compassion on our infirmities, but one tempted in all things like as we are without sin," (Heb. 4), one "able to succour them that are tempted in that wherein He Himself hath suffered and been tempted" (Heb. 2), so we have a Mother and an advocate all the more ready to succour us in our hours of darkness and desolation, in that she herself has suffered the loss of Christ.

6. Mary had no sin to expiate, no evil inclinations to hinder her union with Christ. Yet God, in His loving sympathy for us, decreed that she should suffer a pain we might have thought

impossible to her—weariness in seeking Christ, disappointment, heartsinking, like us, that she might feel for us.

7. "Son, why hast Thou done so to us?" She knows now. When on Calvary she became our Mother, she learned how and why her marvellous power of sympathy had been bought.

8. "Lord, why hast Thou done so to us?" we ask at times when conscience does not reprehend us. And He says to us tenderly, as to Peter: "What I do thou knowest not now, but thou shalt know hereafter."

9. "Why?" Because—apart altogether from the fact that, having lost Him by sin, or the sense of His presence by infidelity, we must painfully seek before we find—there is a reason why even from His faithful servants He hides Himself for awhile:

10. Search is at once a result of love, a trial of love, a purification of love, and the condition of love's reward:

A result of love—"*Quaerens me sedisti lassus.*" Wearily, Lord, hast Thou sought for me; wearily, if Thou wilt, yet constantly I will seek for Thee.

A trial and a purification of love—"How is it that you sought Me?" Have I sought the God of consolation, or the consolations of God?

The condition of love's reward—"Seek and you shall find." "For yet a little, and a very little while and He that is to come will come and will not delay." "Surely I come quickly. Amen. Come, Lord Jesus."

>I thank Thee, Lord, that she who is to soothe
> Our sorest pain,
>Has known the weary search for Christ,
> And search in vain:

> That seeking Him, with Mary we may share
> Our hopes and fears,
> And in the hiding of His Face, take heart
> From Mary's tears.

℣. I sought Him and found Him not:
I called and He did not answer me.—Cant. v.

1. Therefore do I weep, and my eyes run down with water, because the Comforter, the relief of my soul, is far from me.—(Lament. 1.)

2. My tears have been my bread day and night, whilst it is said to me daily: Where is thy God?—(Ps. 41.)

3. Who will grant me that I might find Him? But if I go to the left hand I shall not take hold on Him: if I turn myself to the right hand, I shall not see Him.—(Job 23.)

4. But He knoweth my way, and has tried me as gold that passeth through the fire. My foot hath followed His steps… and the words of His mouth I have hid in my bosom.—(*Ibid.*)

5. I will rise and go about the city: in the streets and the broad ways I will seek Him whom my soul loveth: I sought Him and I found Him not.—(Cant 3.)

6. The watchmen who kept the city found me: Have you seen Him whom my soul loveth?—(*Ibid.*)

7. When I had a little passed by them, I found Him whom my soul loveth: I held Him: and I will not let Him go.—(*Ibid.*)

8. I sat down under His shadow whom I desired.—(Cant. 2.)

9. Show me Thy face, let Thy voice sound in my ears, for Thy voice is sweet and Thy face comely.—(*Ibid.*)

10. My Beloved to me and I to Him…Till the day break and the shadows retire.—(*Ibid.*)

II. The Sorrowful Mysteries

Mary and the Passion

Our Lady is intimately bound up with all the mysteries of our Lord's life on earth. We cannot think of the Infancy or Childhood apart from her. We must not leave her out when we come to the Passion. In the work He came to do for us our Blessed Saviour would have her help throughout. As in His Childhood and in His Public Life, so in His Passion, He associated her with Himself, her tears and prayers and obedience with His own.

Many of His servants have been allowed to follow Him in mysterious companionship through the scenes of His sacred sufferings. What must have been the fellowship vouchsafed to His Mother? He said by His prophet: "There is not a man with Me."—(Isaias 63.) But His Mother was surely with Him; if not actually present always, yet seeing and hearing all that befell Him with a reality reserved for herself alone. She is ready to share her contemplation and her sorrows. What heart so hard as not to desire to share them with her!

Who would visit the scenes of the Passion alone when he could go with Mary! And what a difference it makes in the fruit! How much more deeply the heart is moved, seeing as

Mary sees, feeling as Mary feels! To gain insight into their depths, appreciation of their lessons, love and gratitude to our Lord, and sympathy with Him, we must keep close to her throughout. We must turn continually from the Son to the Mother. In her agonised face we shall see by reflection what He suffers, better than by fixing our gaze on Him alone. Even when she may not be actually present, as at the Agony in the Garden or the mock coronation in the guard-room, we cannot doubt her to have a fuller knowledge of every detail than has been granted to any other. When contemplating any scene, therefore, we may kneel by her side, watch with her eyes, feel through her heart, and come thus "to know our Lord more clearly, to love Him more dearly, and to follow Him more nearly."

Go to her in her lonely room, where on Thursday night she is sharing the Agony of her Son in the Garden and drinking His bitter chalice with Him. Look into her face as she sees Him go to His disciples and humbly ask for their companionship in the loneliness that is upon Him: "Stay you here and watch with Me." O Mother, how willingly wouldst thou stay by His side and keep watch through those hours of awful strife!

See how she trembles as her Son is roughly bound to the pillar. How she notes each dread detail of the preparations. How she shrinks horror-stricken at the sight of the scourge. Look, if you can, into her face as the first strokes fall.

See her anguish when His tormentors press the thorny crown upon His brow. She marks the signs of intolerable pain as they beat it down with the reed. She would bear with joy any agony to bring Him a moment's relief, and she knows that her pain, clearly seen by Him, is an additional torture to

His tender filial Heart. See her tears at the spitting and the mockery.

Ask to go with her on Friday morning as she follows John into the street. The shouts of the crowd on the way to Calvary are his guide where to lead her. Keep close: let not the dense throng separate you from her: you will miss so much of nearness to the Son if you are parted from the Mother. Here at this corner she is to meet Him. Watch the meeting. See the agony of both: their perfect resignation; how they accept what is harder to bear than personal suffering—pain, and shame for that one who is dearer to each than life. Admire these two hearts the most utterly stricken, the meekest, the bravest earth has ever seen.

"*Woman, behold thy son.*" Our Lord had you in His Heart as He hung upon the Cross. The agony of the death throes could not distract Him from your need of an advocate, a comforter, a mother. Faintly from the dry lips came His legacy to you—all He had left to give you, except the life which was ebbing fast: "Son, behold thy Mother." What will you say to Him for there remembering you? What will you say to her for there accepting you? How will you thank God for all the graces that have been the fruit of that commendation?

Mother, dear, all thou canst share with thy children thou art ready to share! Share, then, with me thy pain in the Passion of thy Son. Thou must not keep all for thyself. I have more right to it than thou hast. It was no sin of thine which tore that Flesh, crowned that Head, broke that Heart. "Christ Jesus came into this world to save sinners, of whom I am the chief."—(I. Tim. 1.) "He loved me and delivered Himself for me."—(Galat. 2.)

He redeemed thee, indeed, but with a choice redemption that is for thee alone. His Blood did not ransom thee out of bondage, but kept thee free; did not wash thee from guilt, but made thee immaculate. Therefore, whilst thou didst cost Him much thou wert a joy to Him always. Thy spirit rejoices in God thy Saviour, yet not as ours. And in a higher way than thy children thou dost weep over the sufferings of the Man of Sorrows. Yet thou disdainest not the companionship of the least or the most guilty. With any of us thou wilt share thy pain. Share it now with me.

The Agony in the Garden

I. Behold thou hast taught many, and thou hast strengthened the weary hands…But now the scourge is come upon thee and thou faintest: it hath touched thee and thou art troubled.—Job iv.

THEN Jesus came with them to a country place, Which is called Gethsemane; and He said to His disciples: "Sit you here till I go yonder and pray." And He taketh Peter and James and John with Him, and He began to fear and to be heavy. And He saith to them: "My Soul is sorrowful even unto death; stay you here and watch with Me."

And He was withdrawn from them a stone's cast; and kneeling down He prayed. And He fell upon His face, and He prayed that if it might be, the hour might pass from Him. And

He said: "Abba, Father, all things are possible to Thee; remove this chalice from Me; but not what I will, but what Thou wilt."

And He cometh to His disciples and findeth them asleep. And He said to Peter: "What! couldst thou not watch one hour with Me? Watch ye and pray that ye enter not into temptation. The spirit indeed is willing, hut the flesh is weak."

Again the second time He went and prayed, saying: "My Father, if this chalice may not pass away but I must drink it, Thy will be done." And He cometh again and findeth them asleep, for their eyes were heavy. And leaving them He went away again, and He prayed the third time, saying the same words.

And there appeared to Him an Angel from heaven strengthening Him. And, being in an agony, He prayed the longer. And his sweat became as drops of blood trickling down upon the ground.—(Matth. 26, Mark 14, Luke 22.)

A garden on the western slope of Olivet, close to the brook Kedron that flows through the valley of Jehoshaphat. Olive trees all about. The moon at the full, but the darkness beneath the trees impenetrable. To the north of the garden a grotto fourteen yards by eight or nine. Our Lord prostrate there as in an underground torture chamber. Eight of the Apostles near the garden gate. Peter, James, and John a stone's throw from the scene of the Agony.

According to an ancient tradition, our Lord's first prayer was made under the trees: He withdrew afterwards into the grotto.

II. The sorrows of death encompassed Me,
and the torrents of iniquity troubled Me.—Ps. xvii.

Ponder the words of the Evangelist describing our Lord's state of soul in the Garden: "fear," "heaviness," "agony," "sorrow unto death."

Christ our Lord was not wont to make much of what He did or suffered. He speaks of His Passion as if it were something almost ordinary in the way of pain: "The Son of man shall be delivered to the Gentiles, and shall be mocked and scourged and spit upon and put to death."—(Luke 18.) Hence we must understand Him literally when He speaks of Himself as "sorrowful even unto death." He was enduring the pangs which come upon the soul at the last; when it is being torn from its lifelong companion, the body; when the beads of perspiration stand out thick on the brow of the strong man.

This death-sweat is the evidence of interior torture, and in particular of that awful form of torture—fear. We hear of criminals, on the eve of their execution, suffering in this way. But once or twice only has history recorded that the drops on the brow were blood, the body witnessing thus to the terror that filled the mind. What must have been the anguish of our Lord that night, when from every pore there issued drops of blood, a sweat so copious that after soaking His garments it trickled down upon the ground!

He was given up to a horror and dismay which God in His mercy has spared the vilest sinner. If we would realise it in some faint degree, we must consider what it was to which He offered Himself when He undertook to satisfy for our sins. He was "made sin for us," in the forcible language of the Apostle.—(2 Cor. 5.) The guilt of our sins He could not take, but He took the result of that guilt. He, the All-Holy, drew to Himself all that is loathsome in human sin. He allowed himself to be clad in the foul garment from the contact of which He shrank inexpressibly, and bore the shame of appearing thus before His spotless Court in heaven.

We, on whom sin weighs so lightly, cannot understand what its touch was to Him. But we know that the sensitiveness of the spirit exceeds by far that of the dull flesh. That there is a shrinking from moral defilement, from ingratitude, from shame, more instinctive than any recoil of the senses. But not the most keenly sensitive of us can form any idea of the extent to which pain of body and mind told on the delicate organisation of the Sacred Humanity, framed with a view to its awful office of universal Victim, and supported by Omnipotence to bear the whole weight of the wrath of God, and to satisfy to the full the requirements of His justice.

True, He was offered because it was His own will (Isaias 53). He reminds us again and again that the offering He made in the first moment of His Incarnation was never retracted: "I do not resist: I have not gone back. I have given my body to the strikers, and my cheeks to them that plucked them: I have not turned away my face from them that rebuked me and spat upon me" (Isaias 50). He was so afraid we should see in the petition His anguish wrung from Him a reluctance to suffer for us, that it is almost by stealth we come to know of it. He withdrew even from His three privileged Apostles into the deepest and darkest recesses of the olive grove, into the concealment of the grotto, as if to hide from men the cry of His breaking Heart, which the Father alone would not misconstrue.

Oh yes, He suffered willingly. The very trembling of His spirit and of His flesh bore witness to His devotedness. Only the most intrepid love could have laid itself open to the torture of such fear. Only the absolute determination of His Will could have trusted itself to the violence of such an onslaught.

He suffered willingly. He knelt down to offer Himself for the sins of men, and in an instant the deluge was upon Him. Like a low-lying city whose dykes have given way, His Soul was flooded with the accumulated wickedness of the world. It seemed to identify itself with Him, to be all but His own: "the torrents of iniquity troubled Me" (Ps. 17). Yet there was no vagueness. Each sin stood out clear and distinct, my sin at such an hour, all the sins of my life. And all to be set down to His account, all to be punished in Him as if He were the sinner. O my Lord, what sounding can fathom the depth of Thy humiliation: "Glorious in holiness" (Exod. 15) to be "made sin" for me!

He saw the punishment of the sin He had taken on Himself, and He trembled. He who knows clearly the malice of sin, how should He not tremble at the sight of the expiation due for the sins of the world! The scourge, the nails, the cross, betrayal, mockery, desertion by God and man—all the torture that beginning now was to accumulate and intensify without a moment's respite for soul or body till the last sob on Calvary, was present before Him, vivid and detailed. Well might His Heart quail. For He was true man as one of us. "I also have a heart as well as you" (Job 12). Helpless and unprotected, He lay upon His face, rehearsing all that was to come upon Him, realising, as His Divinity enabled Him to realise, what it was to have been accepted as the Victim for the world's sin. God sustains His martyrs under their torments. Long before the moment when these reach the insupportable, His Providence interferes. Death or unconsciousness comes to the rescue of the fainting flesh. As our English martyrs stepped week after week into the torture chamber, and beheld the preparations, rendered more terrible by familiarity, their trust was in the fidelity of God. They knew in whom they had believed, and they were certain that He would keep that which they had committed to Him—the frail, shrinking flesh, the trembling will. And God never failed His servants. Not one was tried beyond his strength. But there was no such mercy for the Son. He must be stricken to extremity, beyond the point where human nature taxed to its utmost can endure. His Divinity will support Him, not for the alleviation, but for the protraction of His pain. Over the agony of death He is to pass and live on. O sacred suffering Soul, what was my share in Thy intolerable anguish: what has been my return of love to Thee for bearing so much for me!

Pain is sweetened by the thought that it will profit those whom we love. Our Lord saw that for a multitude of souls what He was going to suffer would avail nothing; that they would be lost in spite of all He could do to save them. And of those whom His pains would profit, how many were a drop in His bitter chalice! They would be saved indeed, but how poorly. They would not be obdurate, but they would be niggardly. His self-sacrifice and unstinted generosity would awaken in their souls only the very faintest response. Whilst His constant thought in life and in death had been what more He could do for them, their study would be how little they could do for Him compatible with their own salvation.

There was a last drop in that chalice, one that surpassed in bitterness all that had gone before. If Jerusalem had deserted Him—His own people, His priests: if one apostle was about to betray Him, and all to forsake Him; He had still the Father left Him, the Father's love to make amends for all, the Father's bosom into which to climb. Who could assail Him there? Who should drive Him thence? Oh mystery the more impenetrable the more we search into it—that when He was making to the Divine Majesty an infinite satisfaction, acceptable and accepted, the Father should forsake—it is His own word—treat as a sinner the Son of His love! Because He was made sin for us, because we had deserved to be abandoned by God, Christ was abandoned, a word we should have never dared to use had He not used it first to reveal to us the darkness that gathered round His human Soul, and caused Him anguish beyond which there was nothing left for Him to bear.

This is what we mean by the Agony in the Garden—the throes that must have wrenched asunder soul and body had He not reserved Himself for the death of the Cross. Our agony, O Lord, is but the faintest shadow of Thine. With us it is the forerunner of death close at hand. Thine brought Thee to the gates of death, and held Thee there till the three hours on Calvary were run.

> What drop was mine, my Saviour, in
>   Thy cup of woe,
> Bringing its brimming bitterness
>   To overflow:
>
> What sin of mine oppressed Thy soul
>   With anguish sore
> Driving a death-sweat…and of blood,
>   From every pore?
>
> III. Thou also art wounded as well as we,
> Thou art become like unto us.—Isaias xiv.

The sacred Agony reveals a depth of sympathy and brotherly compassion which we should have thought impossible in a God-man. Had we been asked how our Lord would go forth to meet His torments, we should have said: "With the fearlessness He had ever shown in life when danger threatened, with a dauntless, unruffled soul rejoicing like a giant to run the way, desiring with desire to drain to the dregs the bitter chalice He had resolved to drink for love of us." We should have sent Him into the battle like an earthly captain, animating His followers by His high courage and heroic words. Could we have dreamed of a Leader who, to comfort His terror-stricken soldiers would share their weakness, would be afraid; whose face should blanch, whose voice should tremble as the hour of trial drew on? Could we have brought ourselves to believe that our God would stoop for our sakes to this excess of pitying love? We should have deemed it unworthy of Him. Oh happy was it for us that He had not to take counsel of us! Where should we have gone in our hours of weakness had there been no Gethsemane! What consolation is wanting to us now that we see the mighty God stricken with fear; sickening like us at the sight of failure, treachery, ingratitude; cowering before the anger of God; "with a strong cry and tears offering up prayers and supplications to Him that was able to save Him from death" (Heb. 5).

How practical, how self-forgetting is Christ's love for us! "All that I can do I will do for them" was His motto through life. And thus when His hour came, it was not what best befitted His Majesty, but what would help us most that determined the way in which He would meet suffering and death. To be like His brethren in all things, this was His rule from first to last: that, having shown Himself like us, He may win us to be like Him, ready to say with Him in the hour of trial: "Abba, Father, all things are possible to Thee, let this chalice pass from me. Nevertheless if this chalice may not pass away but I must drink it, Thy Will be done."

IV. My heart is ready.—Ps. lvi.

His hour was come—the hour to which He offered Himself when as a Babe He was presented to His Father in the Temple. The hour of physical torments and of a shameful death, the hour of humiliation and blasphemy, of triumph for His enemies, of agony for His Mother and His friends—that hour had come.

And His hour found Him ready. In the agony of the strife between the flesh and the spirit He sweated blood, for He was truly man. But in spite of repugnance, and darkness, and desolation, He was ready. He stretched out His hands for His chalice: "I do not resist; I have not gone back" (Isaias 50). "My heart is ready, God, My heart is ready" (Ps. 56).

We offer ourselves to Him in a moment of fervour. "Can you drink the chalice I shall drink?" "We can." And when the hour comes to prove our fidelity, to watch and pray and suffer with Him, we are found asleep.

"And they knew not what to answer Him." No indeed, what answer could we make? One only, His own excuse for us: "the spirit is willing but the flesh is weak."

"Strengthen me, O God, in this hour" (Judith 13), is a prayer that should be again and again on our lips in face of a coming trial. Or, better still, our Master's own words: "If this chalice may not pass away but I must drink it, Thy Will be done."

"Can you drink of the chalice I shall drink?" He says to us at times. "Would you like to be very near Me in Heaven, to be among My dearest and most intimate friends for ever and ever? Can you drink of my chalice, then? There is no other way. You may creep into a corner of Heaven if you will. But to go up to its first places there must be close companionship with Me here. Can you find it in your heart to say: 'Give me to drink.'"

Lord, I would be near Thee at any cost, Bid me come to Thee, bid me come close to Thee. With Thy help I will drink of Thy chalice. Thy lips have well nigh drained it, A few drops only Thou hast saved for me, to give me a title to that nearness to Thee that I covet. I will take it from Thy hand: Give me to drink.

V. Like to us in all things.—Heb. iv.

We may think of our Lord as halting between two ways; in a hesitation born of love, as to which of two courses would be most advantageous to us. He had resolved to carry our sorrows, and therefore to know by His own experience the anguish of dejection and fear. But would it be safe to let us see Him in His abasement? Would it scandalize us and shake our faith? That imploring cry: "Father, let this chalice pass from Me," would it make us doubt for an instant His readiness to die for us?

On the other hand, the complete unveiling to us of His human Heart in its weakness and distress, its craving for sympathy, its turning in the hour of trial to those it loved— this would uphold us in our day of sorrow. What would be best for us? What would help us most? Not a thought for Himself or of His own humiliation; absolutely self-forgetting: having loved His own who were in the world, He loved them to the end.

He would risk, then, the trial to their faith. They must have the comfort and encouragement of His companionship in hours of weariness and gloom; they must see Him quailing before the Cross; praying to be spared; creeping to His friends for sympathy and for the protection of their presence in His loneliness and terror. They must see Him turning from the Angel who had never suffered to the human hearts that were like His own. It would involve humiliation such as He had not stooped to as yet. What of that? The law of the Incarnation before all else—like to us in all things excepting sin.

And so He "humbled Himself to us" as the Church says (Collect for Palm Sunday). Is she, too, fearful lest from His prayer in the Garden we should doubt His readiness to suffer and die for us? Any way, she ends every hour of her office in Holy Week with that most touching prayer:

"Look down we beseech Thee, Lord, upon this Thy family, for which our Lord Jesus Christ hesitated not to be betrayed into the hands of sinners and to suffer the torment of the Cross."

"Hesitated not;" never entered into a moment's deliberation about; took it as a matter of course—and this *for me!*

Lessons of the Sacred Agony.

I.

Three days before the Thursday when He was to be sorrowful even unto death, a foretaste of His midnight agony was given Him. It was Palm Sunday. The triumphal procession was over. The Hosannas had ceased, He was healing in the Temple when Peter and Andrew came to tell Him certain Gentiles had come to them with the petition: "We would see Jesus."

How was it that the mention of the Gentiles suggested the Passion? In anguish of spirit, He cried out: "Now is My soul troubled. And what shall I say? Father, save Me from this hour. But for this cause I came unto this hour. Father, glorify Thy name." Here in the Temple Courts as presently in Gethsemane He lets us see the strife—to speak our human language—between the human Will that shrank like ours from torture and disgrace, and the Divine Will that overruled the human and brought it into conformity with Itself.

"*Now is my soul troubled*"—foreseeing the depths of anguish into which it must descend; beholding torments, betrayal, desertion, dereliction, death.

"*What shall I say?*"—to Him to whom all things are possible, who can deliver Me from all the evil that threatens Me?

"*Father, save Me!*"—the cry of a child. Save Me for the love Thou bearest Me, for the trust I place in Thee.

"*From this hour*"—foreseen so long, accepted so fully, yet now that it is at hand beheld with such unspeakable dread.

Here is the voice of the Son of Man, of Him who is like us in all things excepting sin. Here is the human Will swaying in the tempest, yet clinging ever to the Divine.

"*But for this cause I came unto this hour*"—that I might hallow Thy Name, and by My submission prove Myself Thy Son.

"*Father, glorify Thy Name*"—even at My cost, even in the sacrifice of all that as man is dear and precious to Me. In My abasement, in My shame, in the triumph of My enemies, in the desolation of My friends, in the extremity of My pains, in the hiding of Thy face, My Father, a darkness worse than death; by every drop of My blood, by every throb of agony; as in each moment of My life, so in the bitterness of death, Father, glorify Thy Name!

This is our Elder Brother, He who said to us on the eve of His Passion: "I have given you an example that as I have done so you do also." How much of His oblation can we make our own? How deep can we drink of His chalice? He will not ask us to do more than taste what He drained to the dregs. He has proved that He loves us dearly. He has shown us we may trust Him. Shall we not abandon ourselves to Him, and let Him who knows us through and through do with us what He wills!

II.

The chalice which my Father hath given Me shall I not drink it.—John xviii.

It is always my Father's wisdom and love that prepares my chalice, as the physician mingles the draught for his little sick child.

It is always my Father's hand that holds the chalice to my lips. Not this person or that forces it on me, though in the gloom it seems to be so: always, always, it is the chalice that *my Father* hath given me.

It is always my Father's voice that I hear inviting and encouraging me: "Can you drink of the chalice of which I have drunk?" "Take all that shall be brought upon thee, and in thy sorrow endure, and in thy humiliation keep patience" (Ecclus. 2). "What I do thou knowest not now, but thou shalt know hereafter" (John 13). Seek not the things that are too high for thee, and search not into things above thy ability… for it is not necessary for thee to see with thy eyes those things that are hid (Ecclus. 3). "Blessed are they that have not seen and have believed" (John 20).

I will be one of these blessed ones. I will take the chalice from my Father's hand. I will trust in His wisdom and love that have prepared it for me. I will listen to His tender words as He gives me to drink. And in my heart and on my lips shall be those of His well-beloved Son: "Yea, Father, for so hath it seemed good in Thy sight" (Matth. 11). "Not my will but Thine be done" (Luke 22). It shall not be a reproach to me: "They grieved the Holy One, they remembered not His hand. They loved Him with their mouth, but their heart was not right with Him, nor were they counted faithful" (Ps. 77). But "I will take the chalice of salvation and call upon the name of the Lord" (Ps. 115), "and humbly wait for His consolation" (Judith 8).

III.

(1) Believe God and He will recover thee (Ecclus. 2).

(2) Wait on God with patience, join thyself to God and endure (*Id.*).

(3) Take all that shall be brought upon thee; and in thy sorrow endure, and in thy humiliation keep patience (*Id.*).

(4) For He woundeth and cureth; He striketh and His hands shall heal; refuse not therefore the chastising of the Lord (Job 5).

(5) It is the Lord, let Him do what is good in His sight (I. Kings 3).

If it be not He, who is it, then? (Job 9).

(6) Shall not my soul be subject to God? (Ps. 61).

I will bear the wrath of the Lord because I have sinned against Him (Micheas 7).

(7) I am ready, let Him do what is good before Him (II. Kings 15).

(8) Do with me, Lord, according to Thy Will (Tobias 3).

(9) Do all that seemeth good in Thy eyes (I. Kings 14).

(10) Teach me to do Thy Will, for Thou art my God (Ps. 142).

The Scourging at the Pillar

I. From the sole of the foot unto the top of the head there is no soundness therein: wounds and bruises and swelling sores.—Isaias i.

"Then Pilate took Jesus and scourged Him" (John 19). This is all the Scripture tells us of a torture universally admitted to have been worse than death.

See in front of Pilate's hall a large courtyard paved with reddish stones. On its northern side a pillar, two feet and a half in height. Beside the pillar, a step on which the executioner stands to be able to deal his blows with greater force. On the top of the pillar, an iron ring to which our Lord is fastened by His wrists. Note the painfulness of His posture, His body bent, His head bowed down. Look at the scourge, a four-thonged leathern lash, spiked with iron. Each stroke will raise the flesh in bloody furrows, mangling, or cutting it to the bone.

  II. He is our brother and our flesh.—Gen. xxxvii.

 The Scourging is one of those mysteries of humiliation, which, were it not a fact, would be beyond the reach of the most daring imagination to conceive. Being a fact, how does it affect us?

 We come to it again and again in our beads; we give it a thought, perhaps, and pass on, and it has left no impression. How strange this apathy seems! Is there anything to account for it, or to extenuate it? We may hope that He who is ever ready to find excuse for us, will set it down, not wholly to callousness, but to the deadening influence of familiarity, and to the difficulty we have in bringing home to ourselves that He who suffered *was God*. We believe it, but there is little realisation and less response. Another reason for our insensibility may be that in this as in other mysteries of the Passion, we observe indolently, we grudge the labour of examining details. In any case, there is abundant matter for humiliation. We cannot see an animal ill-used without firing up with indignation. Yet we can look unmoved upon the noblest of our race, the Man-God, suffering torture such as this.

 Were it a criminal at the pillar, one who had done us the foulest injury, one who had sought our life, we should be melted into tears of pity at the first stroke of that awful scourge. And it is the Innocent One, who did no sin, our Friend, our Brother, who is pouring out His Blood for us; it is our God, who has assumed our nature to give to His sufferings in that nature an infinite value, whereby to pay the all but infinite debts we have contracted towards Him. It is God who is thus tortured; God who is subjected to this indignity; God who is silent, patient, counting it all joy to suffer thus *for me!*

O God, my Saviour, who for my sake hast borne such agony, such shame, draw my heart to Thee in this most piteous, most touching mystery. Give me a true interior sorrow for my sins, especially for any pampering of my body which has brought Thee to this. Draw me to gratitude and to love, to at least a little appreciation of what Thou didst suffer for me at the pillar. Have patience with the present dulness and coldness of my heart; with the poor return which is all it can now make Thee for Thy love: one day I will pay Thee all.

III. The Lord was angry with Me on your account.—Deut. I

One of the things as to which it behoves us to form a true judgment is surely sin. Yet how hard it is to realise its malice! We know too little of what God is to form any adequate idea of what it is to offend Him. Thus we go through life with a false or very imperfect conception of our relations with Him, and are puzzled about many things of which sin is the only true explanation. If only there were a school in which we could sit down and learn and have brought home to us this terrible evil which we call sin!

Here at the pillar is Christ's school. Here, if anywhere, we may find what we are seeking. Here is an object lesson which may well impress the dullest of us.

"I have given my body to the strikers" (Isaias 50). "I am become as a vessel that is destroyed" (Ps. 30). "The Lord chastising hath chastised me" (Ps. 117).

Why? "Why hath the Lord cast down to the earth the glorious one of Israel?" (Lament. 2).

"He was wounded for our iniquities; He was bruised for our sins; the chastisement of our peace was upon Him, and by His bruises we are healed" (Isaias 53).

It is by pondering its awful havoc on the Person of the Son of God that we come to realise something of the nature of sin. But we must ponder: a hasty glance is of no avail. We must go from wound to wound, from the sole of the foot to the top of the head, and see how there is no soundness in Him, wounds and bruises and swelling sores…"The whole head is sick and the whole heart is sad" (Isaias 1), "because the Lord hath laid on Him the iniquity of us all" (Isaias 53).

My God, give light to my mind that I may see in this mystery what Thy saints have seen, and come to understand and take to heart the lesson given me here at such a cost!

> IV. If in the green wood they do these things, what shall be done in the dry?—Luke xxiii.

An hour hence, our Lord on His way to Calvary will be saying these words to the daughters of Jerusalem. As fitly may He say them to us from the pillar of His scourging. If, in Him "who did no sin" (I. Peter 2), who bore its appearance only, sin is so fearfully chastised, what must we expect who are sinners!

"Lord, dost Thou speak this parable to us or likewise to all," asked Peter, simply, as he sat at his Master's feet on the Mount of Olives, musing on the warning: "Be you also ready, for at what hour you think not the Son of man will come" (Luke 12). Our Lord made answer: "That servant who knew the will of his lord and did not according to his will shall be beaten with many stripes...Unless you do penance you shall all likewise perish" (Luke 13).

"All." Therefore I. Am I ready to meet my Lord? Must I not do penance, the penance of necessity, the penance of prudence, the penance of love? The penance of necessity—repenting of my past sins and confessing them, and shunning all sin and the dangerous occasions of sin? The penance of prudence, not leaving for the fearful expiation of the next life the whole debt of temporal punishment my sins have entailed, but accepting in the spirit of penance the troubles that come to me in the course of God's Providence, and even imposing on myself small privations which, because free, are of great account with God, and go far to satisfy His Justice. The penance of love. "Christ suffered for us, leaving us an example that we should follow His steps" (I. Peter 2). He has not dispensed us from suffering because He has suffered so much. And love for Him will not let us dispense ourselves. St. Paul bids us "fill up those things that are wanting of the sufferings of Christ" (Coloss. 1), the little measure He has left to our love to supply. "Always bearing about in our body the mortification of Jesus" (II. Cor. 4). It is an instinct of love to desire to suffer with the beloved. Hence, great love, great mortification; little love, little mortification; no love, no mortification.

V. I have given my body to the strikers.—Isaias 1.

(1) I see standing at the pillar the most delicately fashioned, the most acutely sensitive of the children of men.

(2) I see Him awaiting the first stroke in an agony of fear, knowing the precise torment each will inflict, up to the point which marks the limit of human endurance, and beyond that

limit where His Divinity is to sustain Him for the protraction of His pain.

(3) I see His shrinking shame, more intolerable than any physical torture.

(4) I note how He looks around for a friendly face, a sign of recognition, pity, sympathy. And in vain: "I looked for one that would grieve together with me, and there was none" (Ps. 68).

(5) I see, as the first strokes fall, the flesh quiver, the head fall on the breast, the breath come quick and short. The anguish is unendurable. But He thinks of me and nerves Himself to suffer still more.

(6) I mark the deep wounds as the scourging proceeds; so deep that in many places the bones are laid bare. Towards the end of the hour the sacred body is but one sore.

(7) The cords are cut and He falls to the ground. I see Him summoning up the little strength left Him, to seek His garments thrown here and there. No one to do Him even this service. No one to pity Him. His arms are so weak that He can scarcely lift the seamless robe over His head. It adheres to the raw flesh on every side, and at every movement causes Him unspeakable torture.

O God, my Saviour, what must my soul be worth to have been bought at such a price! For I know the meaning of this awful scene. It is to expiate my sensuality that Thou art so shamefully used. It is to win me to sorrow for my sins by showing me the punishment they have deserved. What ought I to do after this? Can I see Thee making such reparation for me and not desire to make some satisfaction myself? If I cannot look out for occasions, shall I not at least bear bodily suffering with patience and unite my pain with Thine?

VI. By His bruises we are healed. —Isaias liii.

O wounds that such a healing need!
O healing that a God must bleed
   And agonise to win!

O ye whose peace His stripes shall earn,
Round the red pillar throng, to learn
   The awfulness of sin!

VII. I am become as a man without help.—Ps. lxxxvii.

(1) I looked for one that would grieve together with me, but there was none: and for one that would comfort me, and I found none (Ps. 68).

(2) There is no one that hath regard to my soul (Ps. 141).

(3) Friend and neighbour thou hast put far from me, and my acquaintance, because of misery (Ps. 87).

(4) My familiar friends are departed from me (Job 6).

(5) I looked on my right hand and beheld, and there was no one that would know me (Ps. 141).

They that knew me have forgotten me…and he whom I loved most is turned against me (Job 19).

(6) Go your way, my children, go your way, for I am left alone (Baruch 4).

(7) I am forgotten as one dead from the heart (Ps. 30).

(8) O all ye that pass by the way, attend and see if there be any sorrow like to my sorrow (Lament. 1).

(9) Have pity on me, have pity on me, at least you my friends, for the hand of the Lord hath touched me (Job 19).

(10) Attend to my supplication, for I am brought very low (Ps. 141).

The Crowning with Thorns

i. I looked for one that would grieve together with me, but there was none: and for one that would comfort me, and I found none.—Ps. lxviii.

THEN the soldiers of the governor, taking Jesus into the hall, gathered together unto Him the whole band, and, stripping Him, they clothe Him with purple. And platting a crown of thorns, they put it upon His head, and a reed in His right hand. And bowing the knee before Him, they began to salute Him, (and) they mocked Him, saying: "Hail! King of the Jews." And spitting upon Him, they took the reed and struck His head (Matth. 27, Mark 15, John 19).

See the barrack-yard of the soldiers in the Praetorium. The whole band, about five hundred men, gathered together for the sport. Our Lord seated on a stone bench. An old scarlet cloak about His shoulders. On His head a crown, *i.e.*, a raised cap or mitre, of thorns, covering the whole head and half of the forehead, the long, sharp thorns protruding inside and outside. In His hand a reed. Streams of blood trickling down His face and through His hair, filling His eyes and beard.

See the soldiers marching before Him, genuflecting as they pass: every now and then a halt to offer Him some fresh insult; some spitting on Him, some striking Him, all mocking Him.

Hear the shouts, the laughter, the uproar, the blasphemy. Hear the silence of Christ.

> II. They are not afraid to spit in my face.—Job xxx.

Pity our Lord as He goes from the pillar of the Scourging to the scene of His next torment. Wonder that human hearts could be so hard, that hatred could be so relentless as not to be satisfied with the state to which the Scourging has brought Him. See His tottering steps. He is exhausted with pain and loss of blood. Every movement is torture. His woven tunic is clinging to a body that is one wound. The soldiers push Him before them to the barrack-yard, where they are going to have some sport by dressing Him up as a king, and doing Him mock homage.

See them roughly taking off His vesture; not even His Mother could have removed it without causing Him exquisite torture. They seat Him on a low stone bench, throw a red rag round His shoulders by way of a royal mantle, and put a reed in His hand for a sceptre. A crown alone is wanting. One of them has seen a thick briar growing near the door. It would serve the purpose. They cut a branch covered with hard spikes, and, taking care not to hurt their hands, twist it into a kind of helmet bristling with sharp points within and without. They put it on to His Head and beat it down with the reed.

Mark His agony as the thorns are driven into the eyes, into the temples, into the nerves. See the rush of tears caused by the intolerable pain. The blood trickles through His hair, disfigures His face, fills and blinds His eyes.

Now begins the mockery. They draw themselves up in line and pass before Him, bowing the knee and saluting Him: Hail! King of the Jews." One takes the reed from His hand and strikes His head. Others pull His beard and buffet Him. He makes no resistance. There is no sign of indignation. He does not turn away His face when they spit upon Him. When they want the reed to strike His head, He gives it them, and takes it into His trembling hand when they return it to Him. He endures beyond the limit of endurance, because supported by His Divinity, torture that would have killed the strongest man. His physical suffering is awful, but it is not the worst. Think what He feels in that tender, sensitive Heart of His!

"Spitting upon Him." This indignity was not only foreseen by the prophet, but was one of the few pains of the Passion foretold by Himself. "The Son of man shall be betrayed and delivered to the Gentiles, and shall be mocked, and scourged, and spit upon, and put to death." Six only of His sufferings mentioned out of so many, and among these the mockery and the spitting! He was a king, and He felt as none but a king could feel dishonour, treachery, betrayal. "For this is God, our God unto eternity, and for ever and ever" (Ps. 47). "The blessed and only mighty, the King of kings and Lord of lords" (I. Tim. 6). How, then, will He feel the outrage He endures at the hands of a brutal soldiery!

His Angels surround Him in adoration and astonishment. This is the treatment He receives from the human family, which He has preferred to them, which He has honoured so unspeakably by making it His own! How they marvel at the predilections of God, and try to see what He sees in this human race that is being redeemed in so wondrous a way, at such tremendous cost.

> III. In what place soever thou shalt be, lord my king, either in death, or in life, there will thy servant be.—2 Kings xv.

Which of us will have the courage to say this as we kneel before our King crowned with thorns? Who will desire to have it said of him: "Thou also wast with Jesus of Nazareth in humiliation and disgrace?" Thousands of His saints have been thus loyal. But we maintain that not having the grace of the saints we are not called to imitate them in this respect. So close a following of the King is to be admired rather than imitated. Discretion is not a virtue only, but a duty. We have our position to uphold, and so far from permitting us to submit to anything in the shape of dishonour, it requires us to act on the maxim: "No one shall provoke me with impunity."

Still, as I kneel before Christ crowned with thorns, my King, as well as the King of all saints, my Leader no less than theirs, a sense of disquiet comes over me, a feeling of being out of harmony with Him in His meekness and patience under injury, He may not want me to endure outrage, but

He does ask me to pass over a slight, to bear peacefully the annoyances of daily life, the failings or the inconsiderateness of those around me. Can I dispense myself from following Him at least thus far, and still call myself His disciple?

How can I get the fortitude to follow Him more closely? For it is fortitude that is wanting. It is the feeble-minded who stand up hotly for their rights, whom no one can provoke with impunity. Where can I get the royal virtue of meekness, the greatness and strength of soul to bear at least the little rubs of life as I ought?

Let me look into the Heart of my King as He sits there, the sport of the vilest rabble. What sustains Him? What makes Him suffer willingly in spite of the repugnance of nature? The same recognition of the Father's hand in all that befalls Him, to which His words in the Garden testified: "The chalice that My Father hath given Me, shall I not drink it?" The faith that sees the Father's hand in every trial, this it is that holds the secret of meekness. To it alone belongs the strength of endurance, the peacefulness of trust. A faith such as this transforms the aspect of life. It gives a charmed life that disaster and the malice of men assail in vain.

We cannot doubt that every event in the life of the Son of God came about by the express decree or by the permission of God. The same is true of all events in our own lives, those included in which the human element is most apparent. If, instead of ascribing my troubles to chance or to the ill-will of others, I rise to the thought of God's designs in sending them, I shall find myself in a region of calm. I shall have passed beyond the reach of the sting that comes from the hand of man, but is not found in the hand of my Father who is in heaven.

Pain, indeed, comes from that hand, but for a little while only. It gives the trial that it may be able to give the reward; the crown of thorns to-day, the crown of glory to-morrow. Meanwhile, pain is sweetened by the thought that my companionship with Him here and hereafter softened His sorrows to my King the day He bore them in meekness and in love for me.

IV. *Jesus therefore came forth bearing the crown of thorns.* —John xix.

> Say, will that thorn-crowned Head
>   As members own
> The delicately bred?
>   Shall it alone
> Languish, and smart, and bleed?
>   Or, rather, shall they miss
> Not following its lead
>   Its everlasting bliss?

V. *You are bought with a great price.*—I Cor. i.

See our Lord seated there, meek, brave, invincible in His patience. On every side the thorns encircle and pierce His head, wounding the temples, breaking the nerves. This in expiation of our evil thoughts; our pride, rebellion, contempt of authority, uncharitable interpretations. This to teach us how to bear headache, anxiety, worry.

See His face, defiled with spittle, besmeared with blood, swollen and bruised with blows a fearful sight to look upon. From their intolerable pain, His half-closed eyes have all but lost the power of sight. Dimly through tears and blood they discern the long line of mockers, and the hand lifted to snatch the reed and beat the crown still deeper into the head. This in atonement for our vanity, our curiosity, our love of display.

His parched, pallid lips, His shoulders seamed with the

lash, His trembling limbs, His aching Heart, all these are bearing the penalty our sinful flesh has deserved. He loved me and delivered Himself for me.

O my King, can I resist this piteous sight! Can I see unmoved what my sins have brought upon Thee! Can I refuse Thee my gratitude and my love! I was not by the pillar of the Scourging nor in the bar rack-yard. I could not tell Thee of my thankfulness at the time Thou didst suffer for me. But how frightful would be my ingratitude were I to show myself ungrateful now! Who shall pay my debt if I neglect it? My pity for Thee in Thy pains, my sorrow for my cruel sins that caused them, is as acceptable to Thee now as it would have been at the hour when Thou wert enduring all this for me.

But if my gratitude is to be more than a name, I must seek out and destroy the cause of Thy sufferings. I must look at the Model Thou hast set before me, and reform myself by what I see there.

"Who when He was reviled did not revile" (I. Peter 2).

Do I pray for grace to forgive what I cannot forget?

Do I practise self-control when I feel hurt?

Do I try to accept bitterness of speech with sweetness?

Do I make allowance for mistakes and misunderstanding, and strive to accommodate myself to those of a different character from my own?

Am I too exacting?

Am I ready to make sacrifices for the sake of peace?

Am I as quick to find excuse for others as for myself?

Am I royally merciful towards those I dislike, or who dislike me?

Do I make others impatient by contradiction?

Do I check in myself the spirit of criticism?

VI. The Lord hath cast down and hath not spared all that was beautiful.—Lament. ii.

(1) God hath delivered me into the hands of the wicked (Job 16).

(2) My enemies have surrounded me: they have set their eyes bowing down to the earth (Ps. 16).

(3) They have opened their mouths upon me, and reproaching me, they have struck me on the cheek (Job 16).

(4) 1 am made a derision to all my people (Lament. 3).

(5) They abhor me, and are not afraid to spit in my face (Job 30).

(6) I am turned in my anguish whilst the thorn is fastened (Ps. 31).

(7) 1 shall not lift up my head, being filled with affliction and misery (Job 10).

(8) My shame is before me: and the confusion of my face hath covered me (Ps. 43).

(9) O my people, what have I done to thee, or in what have I molested thee? Answer thou me. (Micheas 6).

VII. Art thou a king, then? I am a king. For this was I born, and for this came I into the world.—John xviii.

(1) Come, let us adore and fall down and weep before the Lord that made us, for He is the Lord our God (Ps. 94).

(2) Bring to the Lord glory and honour (Ps. 28).

(3) All the Gentiles shall adore in His sight (Ps. 21).

(4) All the kings of the earth shall adore Him, all nations shall serve Him (Ps. 71).

(5) All the nations Thou hast made shall come and adore before Thee, Lord, and they shall glorify Thy name (Ps. 85).

(6) Let all the earth adore Thee and sing to Thee (Ps. 65).

(7) Thou alone art the God of all the kingdoms of the earth (Isaias 37).

(8) Thou art worthy, O Lord our God, to receive glory, and honour, and power (Apoc. 4).

(9) To Jesus Christ our Lord be glory and magnificence, empire and power, before all ages, and now, and for all ages of ages, Amen (Jude 1).

(10) For of Him, and by Him, and in Him are all things: to Him be glory for ever. Amen (Romans 11).

The Carrying of the Cross

I. And bearing His own cross He went forth.—John xix.

AND after they had mocked Him, they took off the purple from Him, and put His own garments on Him, and they led Him out to crucify Him.

And bearing His own cross He went forth.

And there were also two other malefactors led with Him to be put to death.

And as they led Him away, they laid hold of one Simon of Cyrene coming from the country, the father of Alexander and of Rufus; and they laid the cross on him to carry after Jesus.

And there followed Him a great multitude of people and of women, who bewailed and lamented Him. But Jesus turning to them said: "Daughters of Jerusalem, weep not over Me, but weep for yourselves and for your children...For if in the green wood they do these things what shall be done in the dry?"

And they bring Him into the place called Golgotha, which being interpreted, is the place of Calvary (Matth. 27, Mark 15, Luke 23, John 19).

See the Praetorium of Pilate, and to the west, at a distance of about three-quarters of a mile, Calvary. The road descending from the Praetorium into the Tyropean Valley, then climbing a steep ascent to the Gate of Judgment. "The place of Calvary" at a short distance outside the Gate.

See the streets through which the procession is to pass—dark, narrow, dirty, roughly paved with large stones, here and there crossed by arches.

See the multitudes come up for the Pasch lining the whole length of the road. Eager sight-seers in every doorway, on every roof.

Watch the procession coming from the Praetorium—the centurion on horseback taking the lead; a herald walking beside him; the thieves, filled with rage and despair; our Lord tottering under His heavy load, His right hand trying to steady the cross on His shoulder, His left to gather His long robe from under His feet. Around the prisoners, executioners, soldiers, priests, Pharisees, a vast crowd insulting them, children throwing stones at them.

See the ladders, ropes, and nails.

Notice there, at a corner of the street, the Blessed Mother with Magdalen and John.

Hear the babel of sounds—the herald proclaiming the sentence; the tongues of every nation under heaven; the yells, jeers, blasphemy of the crowds; hear on every side the words:

"impostor," "seducer," "blasphemer."

> II. I have given you an example that as I have done, so you do also.—John xiii.

Our Lord accepts His cross at the time and in the shape in which it is presented to Him.

He does not examine it, but embraces it.

He does not consider the cruelty of those who lay it upon Him, but the love of the Father who has chosen it for Him.

He does not complain of its weight, or seek to cast it upon others, but summons up all His strength to bear it.

He accepts, not only the cross itself, but all the painful circumstances that accompany it.

If He is relieved of His burden for a time, it is not by His own act. He is grateful for the relief, but readily accepts the load when it is laid on Him anew.

His heavy cross does not make Him unmindful of the lesser sorrows of others, or unsympathising, or ungracious. He will stop on His road to Calvary to speak to the women of Jerusalem, to greet His Mother at least by a look, to reward Veronica, to thank the Cyrenean.

He will not come down from His cross when defied by His enemies, but only at the bidding of His Father.

He will be taken down by the hands of others when His work is finished; the last pang endured; the Will of Him who sent Him fully accomplished.

Does my way of bearing my cross show that I have studied my Master on His way to Calvary?

> III. Come thou also with thy servants. He answered: I will come. So he went with them.—4 Kings vi.

The disciples of Eliseus with a toilsome journey before them asked for their master's company as encouragement.

Could the servants of God do the like? Had we stood by the smoking Mount of Sinai and seen the lightnings and the flames, and heard the thunders and "the noise of the trumpet exceeding loud," and the voice of the Lord speaking, should we not have cried out with the children of Israel: "Let not the Lord speak to us lest we die"? Would the boldest of us have dared to ask for the intimate presence of that God of majesty in our midst? That He should be a wayfarer like ourselves through the desert, our Elder Brother, our Pioneer, going before us to point out and smoothe the way?

The Incarnation has done for us what we could not have asked or imagined. It has brought Him down among us. The God of Sinai is toiling along the dusty road. He is bent beneath His burden, faint, footsore, weary. Why? Because His servants, His brethren, are on that painful path. Where we are He must be with us. The cry of our heart to the God who made us was: "Come Thou also with Thy servants." He answered: "I will come." So He went with them.

IV. In all things like as we are, without sin.—Heb. iv.

Is there anything so disheartening on the road to heaven as the repeated falls that follow upon our best resolutions! We know they should not cast us down as they do. They are not without their advantages. They teach us self-knowledge. They incite us to humility and contrition. They serve as a stimulus to greater fidelity and fervour in the future. On the other hand, discouragement does more harm than the fall itself. Its source and its fruits are distinctly bad. It springs from pride, for if we knew ourselves better we should be less surprised to find ourselves so weak. It aggravates the evil done in the past. It weakens us for the future. All this we have been told a hundred times. We believe it, we have experienced it, and—we remain discouraged.

Hast Thou any better comfort for us, dear Master, anything that comes home to us more in those moments of depression when we are too weary to reason, too sad to seek a remedy? Thou art wont to come down to the level of our miseries, and lighten them by taking them upon Thyself. Canst Thou do this here? Was it for our encouragement that in spite of Thine efforts to reach Calvary Thou didst stumble and fall again and again? Fall as we fall, Thou couldst not. But the contrivances of Thy love bring Thee marvellously near to us. In Thy desire to show Thyself our Brother, like to us in all things excepting sin, Thou dost take appearances where Thou mayst not take the reality. Thou dost suffer the effects of guilt as Thou canst not incur its stain. Thou art like us, O Son of Man, in our sorrows; like us, O Holy One, in the sadness that comes of sinfulness; like us, O mighty God, in our fears!

O dear Lord Jesus, how touching is Thy faltering and failing on the uphill road! How reassuring is it for us, Thy weak brethren, to creep up to Thee after our own falls, and see Thee lying prostrate, spent, powerless. And—here is our example—whilst still trembling with the shock and pain of Thy fall, with all the weariness of failure upon Thee, with the knowledge that at no great distance Thy strength will give way anew—rising and struggling on, in no wise shaken in Thy resolve to pursue Thy way, and to prove by Thy very falls Thy unconquerable love of us.

In many things I am too weak to follow Thee, dear Lord. But on the toilsome path of daily duty my very weakness makes me like Thee. I fall, oh how many times! My falls bring with them soreness, dejection, the temptation to give up the struggle. But this with the help of Thy grace I will never do. I will remember Thou art at hand still, the same yesterday, to-day, and for ever; indulgent, easily appeased, ready to forgive. Thou dost deplore far more than I do anything like estrangement between us, and only waitest for me to turn to Thee with my "Peccavi" to put all right again. The mother whose little one has fallen and bruised itself, does not beat or even blame it, but runs at its first cry and kisses the sore place, and makes it well. Her instinct is God-given. But tenderer still is the love of the Divine Heart Itself. "He will have compassion on thee more than a mother" (Ecclus. 4). This shall be my consolation, Lord. I will think more of Thy mercy than of Thy justice, of having disappointed than of having displeased Thee. I will even count on a kind of fellow-feeling with me in my falls, and look to Thee who didst stumble and fall on the road to Calvary, to pity me and help me again on my way. After Thy example I will rise at once and trudge on by Thy side as before, trusting to Thy more abundant grace. By Thy weakness, O Lord, strengthen me. By Thy weariness refresh me. By Thy perseverance uphold me to the end. Give me the trust in Thee that holds on its way, undismayed by slips and by bruises, fixed in its resolution to reach Thee at last. Thou art watching, waiting, stretching out Thy arms to me. Draw me into their embrace when life is done, and reward throughout eternity by the possession of Thyself a trust that has never failed.

In Thee, Lord, have I hoped, I shall never be confounded (Ps. 30).

V. They laid the cross on him to carry after Jesus.—Luke xxiii.

It was for Simon's sake much more than for His own that our Lord shared His cross with him. The virtue that came from its contact with the Son of God went out to him who was following in His footsteps. Quickly he learned his lesson. From bearing the cross reluctantly, he came to bear it patiently, willingly, joyfully, reaching thus the highest perfection of which love is capable on earth.

To carry after Jesus. With Him toiling on in front, it was not hard to follow. He had taken the galling weight from the cross when He bore it on His shoulder.

They laid the cross on him. True, but did Simon stop at the instruments? When, after years spent in his Master's service, he looked back to the meeting on the road to Calvary, did he so much as think of the hands that constrained him? Was not the hand of God too plain? Was it not God who planned that meeting, who chose him for the honour of being the first to carry the cross after Jesus?

Looking back on their lives from the bed of death and from their place in heaven, the servants of God see that what they could least spare out of their life would be its crosses. It is the cross that has stamped them all with the mark special to the elect. "For whom He foreknew He also predestinated to be made conformable to the image of His Son" (Rom. 8).

How wonderful are God's dealings with us! How continually He turns our days of trouble into times of richest blessing! The thieves led out of prison on the first Good Friday to die with our Lord, looked on that day as the most miserable in their lives, whereas it was to bring them an offer of mercy and happiness such as they had never had before.

A grace was preparing for them strong enough to set right all that was wrong and bring them, after a few hours of sorrow, into eternal joy.

Little did Simon of Cyrene suspect that Friday morning as he went forth to his daily toil, that grace was lying in wait for him on the road to Calvary; that hidden in the cross of pain and shame was laid up for him the highest honour and never-ending joy!

We rise in the morning and make our plans for the day. God has made His for us. Turning a corner, we find the cross of Christ awaiting us, and with it the grace that with a little effort on our part will enable us to bear it bravely after our Master. How is it that whilst we have plenty of congratulations for Simon, we have nothing but compassion for ourselves!

Teach me, dear Lord, to bear my crosses with faith, and hope, and love. With faith—to believe they come from Thy hand, to cry out when I see one in the distance: "It is the Lord!" With hope—because if I follow Thee to Calvary now, I shall follow Thee into Thy Kingdom by and by. With love—that will make me glad to bear something for Thee who hast borne so much for me.

VI. And bearing His own cross He went forth.—John xix.

> Who but Himself might such a burden bear!
>   All weariness, all woe concentred there:
> Framed for Christ's dauntless charity alone,
>   Uneased, unshared, in very truth—His own.
>
> Weighed, Lord and Master, with Thy load of pain,
>   How light the servant's lot! yet I complain:
> Up, coward heart! shoulder thy cross and cry:
>   "Let us, too, go with Him to bleed and die."

VII. In death they were not divided.—2 Kings i.

Our Lord has taught us many a lesson in His journeyings up and down the land of Judea during the years of His Ministry. On His way to Calvary He must teach us at every turn, for His time is short. His Blessed Mother, too, the first and most faithful of His disciples, is to serve us for an example on the Way of the Cross. They have a lesson for us at the corner of this street where they are to meet.

Let us watch the meeting and see the kind of consolation they bring to one another in this hour of bitter anguish for both. What fortitude! What forgetfulness of self! What control of the strongest, holiest affection earth has ever seen by the all-absorbing thought of the Will of God! Mary's heart beats in perfect unison with the Heart of her Son. Like His, it throws itself into the Divine Will for the redemption of the world with a strength of purpose that overmasters the instincts of nature.

See them! Listen! There is no shrinking in their self-immolation, no lamentation at the sight of the anguish of the one dearer to each than life. The Son and the Mother meet, but it is as the Redeemer and the Co-Redemptrix of the world. The Sacrifice their sublime office demands occupies them entirely. Their eyes meet. Dimly, through the tears and blood that obscure His sight, our Lord discerns His Mother's face, and His glance carries strength to her soul. He summons her, His well-beloved, to ratify the oblation made at Nazareth in the hour of the Incarnation, when she consented to become the Mother of the Man of Sorrows; the oblation made solemnly in the Temple on the day of His Presentation, and renewed again and again as the time of the

Passion drew near: "Behold the handmaid of the Lord." At every stage of His Redemption she is His handmaid, waiting upon Him always, His fellow-worker on whose sympathy and absolute fidelity He can rely.

And now His hour has come; the hour of which He had so often spoken to her at Nazareth; the hour that was the subject of such earnest prayer put up together as they knelt there side by side; the hour for which He had promised to strengthen her, that, first in privilege as in dignity, she might drink deeper than any other of His chalice. His glance recalls all this to her now.

And it is met by a response such as that handmaid alone could give. No cry of pain escapes her. To bring Him the only comfort in her power—the assurance that she accepts with Him every jot and tittle of the Father's Will; that she does not grudge one pang; that she is ready for more, for the consummation of the Sacrifice, for Calvary—this is her one thought. She cannot speak her "*Ecce ancilla.*" Her heart would break with a word to Him. But her eyes, her quivering lip, her clasped hands speak for her. It is but for a moment that the Son and the Mother meet. Yet in that moment are rehearsed the thoughts and desires and resolves of the Three-and-Thirty Years.

I turn to myself. What kind of consolation do I bring to my friends in the path of daily life that is for so many the Way of the Cross? Is it a help to them, a spiritual support to meet me?

Do I try to take the sting out of wounds, or are they the worse for my handling?

Do I by injudicious sympathy accentuate vexations or misunderstandings?

If I listen to angry words, is it with the view of relieving an overcharged heart, and of saying a soothing and helpful word later?

Do I try to put a favourable construction on painful words or acts, and abstain from repeating what would work further mischief?

Do I ever speak to my friends of finding light, strength, remedy in prayer? "And Jonathan went to David and strengthened his hands in God" (I. Kings 23). Are my friends moved by my words to bear up bravely, to trust in God, "and humbly wait for His consolation"? (Judith 8).

In a word, have I studied the meeting of Jesus and Mary on the road to Calvary and learned how true friendship comports itself in the hour of trial?

VIII. Thou also wast with Jesus of Nazareth.—Mark xiv.

Thou wert glad, dear Lord, to suffer for me. Not that Thou couldst desire suffering for its own sake for Thou wert truly man, and Thine exquisitely sensitive nature shrank as none other ever shrank from pain. But Thou didst long to go through that pain which was to purchase my happiness and to prove Thy love to me. If Thou didst look forward with eagerness to Thy Passion, it was for my sake.

So must it be with me. I cannot desire suffering for itself. But with the grace which Thou wilt give to me as to Thy saints I may come to love that which will bring me nearer to Thee; will forward Thy designs for my sanctification and happiness; will enable me to glorify Thee more; will be proof to Thee of my gratitude and my love. We speak of the *sign* of the Cross. I can love the Cross at least inasmuch as it is a sign to heaven and earth, to angels and to men, to Thee, my God, and to myself, that I am on Thy side, that I belong to Thee, that I am marked here with that seal which is to be the salvation of the elect on the last tremendous Day: "Hurt not the earth, nor the sea, nor the trees, till we sign the servants of our God in their foreheads." O Lord, when Thou dost send me the Cross here to give me a right to bear it hereafter, let me not turn away rebellious or disconsolate. Let me not sorrow as those that have no hope, bitterly because unwillingly. I shall be so glad, so proud on the Last Day to bear the Cross on my forehead, to hear the congratulations of the saints: "Thou also wast with Jesus of Nazareth." Why should I not feel at least the beginnings of that gladness now?

> IX. Christ suffered for us leaving you an example that you should follow His steps.—I Peter ii.

(1) Whither I go you know and the way you know (John 14).

(2) If any man will come after Me, let him deny himself, and take up his cross daily, and follow Me (Luke 9).

(3) He that taketh not up his cross and followeth Me, is not worthy of Me (Matth. 10).

(4) The disciple is not above the master, nor the servant above his lord (*Id.*).

(5) It is enough for the disciple that he be as his master, and the servant as his lord (*Id.*).

(6) Come to Me all you that labour and are burdened, and I will refresh you (Matth. 11).

(7) Take up My yoke upon you and learn of Me because I am meek and humble of heart, and you shall find rest to your souls (*Id.*).

(8) Master, I will follow Thee whithersoever Thou shalt go (Matth. 8).

(9) Go whither thou wilt and I will be with thee (I. Kings 14).

(10) In what place soever thou shalt be, lord my king, either in death or in life, there will thy servant be (II. Kings 15).

The Crucifixion

I. Jesus Christ who hath loved us and washed us from our sins in His own blood.—Apoc. i.

And they bring Him into the place called Golgotha, which being interpreted, is the place of Calvary. And they gave Him to drink wine mingled with myrrh. And when He had tasted He would not drink.

And it was the third hour and they crucified Him…And with Him they crucified the robbers, one on the right hand and the other on the left, and Jesus in the midst…

And Jesus said: "Father, forgive them, for they know not what they do…"

And the people stood beholding. And they that passed by blasphemed Him, wagging their heads and saying: "Vah!

Thou that destroyest the Temple of God, and in three days dost rebuild it, save Thy own self. If Thou be the Son of God, come down from the cross…"

And one of those robbers who were hanged, blasphemed Him, saying: "If Thou be Christ, save Thyself and us." But the other answering, rebuked him, saying: "Neither dost thou fear God, seeing thou art under the same condemnation? And we indeed justly, for we receive the due reward of our deeds, but this Man hath done no evil." And he said to Jesus: "Lord, remember me when Thou shalt come into Thy Kingdom." And Jesus said to him: "Amen, I say to thee, this day thou shalt be with Me in Paradise."

Now there stood by the cross of Jesus, His Mother, and His Mother's sister, Mary of Cleophas, and Mary Magdalen. When Jesus, therefore, had seen His Mother, and the disciple standing whom He loved, He saith to His Mother: "Woman, behold thy son." After that He saith to the disciple: "Behold thy Mother." And from that hour the disciple took her to his own.

And it was almost the sixth hour. And when the sixth hour was come, there was darkness over the whole earth until the ninth hour.

And at the ninth hour Jesus cried out with a loud voice, saying: "*Eloi, Eloi, lamma sabacthani!*" Which is, being interpreted: "My God! My God! why hast Thou forsaken me?

Afterwards Jesus, knowing that all things were now accomplished, that the Scripture might be fulfilled, said: "I thirst." Now there was a vessel set there full of vinegar; and immediately one of them running, took a sponge and filled it with vinegar, and putting it upon a reed, put it to His mouth, and gave Him to drink.

Jesus, therefore, when He had taken the vinegar, said: "It is consummated."

And Jesus again crying with a loud voice, said; "Father, into Thy hands I commend my spirit."

And saying this, and bowing His head, He gave up the ghost.

And the earth quaked, and the rocks were rent, and the graves were opened, and many bodies of the saints that had slept, arose, and coming out of the tombs after His Resurrection, came into the holy city and appeared to many.

And they that were watching Jesus, having seen the earthquake and the things that were done, were sore afraid, saying: "Indeed, this was the Son of God." And all the multitude of them that were come together to that sight, and saw the things that were done, returned striking their breasts (Matth. 27. Mark 15. Luke 23. John 19).

See Calvary and the surrounding country at the beginning of the three hours. Amid the gathering darkness, the three crosses facing west. The figures of the crucified standing out white and gaunt in the gloom.

Watch the immense concourse moving up towards the central cross. Notice how the priests, Pharisees, and ancients go among the people, stirring them up to revile Him who hangs there. See group after group of the priests coming to the cross, looking up, wagging their heads in mockery. Observe the soldiers keeping guard, and casting lots for His poor garments. At a little distance our Lady, St. John, and the holy women.

Hear the jeers, reproaches, blasphemies of the priests, their thanksgiving to God who has delivered the nation from this seducer. Hear them quieting the people frightened by the darkness. Hearken to our Lord saying: "Father, forgive them."

See, during the next hour, the earth in darkness; the space round the cross free; the enemies of Christ, fearful and uneasy, seeking their homes; the people, terrified, gathered together in groups, looking in silence towards the Crucified; the centurion and his band in reverent attitudes; the Blessed Mother and her companions standing beneath the cross.

Hear the people speaking in whispers; talking of our Lord's miracles and goodness; saying, "He hath done all things well"; pitying Him; praising Him; condemning their rulers. Hear the words of the thieves; our Lord's words to the good thief and to His Mother. Hear Him saying: "I thirst."

See, during the third hour, the Mount becoming deserted; the multitude going away striking their breasts; the sacred Body drooping towards the earth. Mary still standing, still gazing upwards, waiting for the end.

See the veil of the Temple torn asunder; the rocks rent; the tombs opened; the dead rising.

Hear the stillness round the cross as the ninth hour draws on; the last words of our Lord; the loud cry with which His Soul goes forth.

> II. And I, if I be lifted up from the earth,
> will draw all things to Myself. —John xii.

See Jerusalem on the day of the Crucifixion. About two millions of people in and around the city. Look at the crowds winding through the dark, narrow thoroughfares, pouring through the Judgment Gate, and congregating in vast masses round the place of execution. Watch the three condemned as they painfully toil up the little mound outside the walls known as "the place of Calvary." The soldiers clear a space on the summit. The crosses are thrown on the ground. The executioners lay hands on our Lord.

How tenderly we prepare for death those whom we love! What circumspection there is in our words, what care to banish sights and sounds that would disturb, to provide what may soothe, to soften in every way love can suggest the terrible parting of soul and body!

Our Lord is prepared for death by His executioners. He has been made to carry His cross. All the dread preparations are made before His eyes and those of His Mother. There is no pity, no attempt to mitigate in the very least the awful sentence of crucifixion. The drink offered by custom to the condemned to lessen their pain, is mixed with gall for Him. The crown of thorns has been so knocked about, so roughly removed and replaced, that His head is a mass of wounds. His sacred body is but one sore, not the lightest texture could touch it without causing Him exquisite pain. Is it in expiation of our vanity that He would have His vesture during the whole of His Passion a source of torture to Him? The sweat of blood in the Garden that trickled down to the ground must have first saturated His garments. Think how hard and stiff they would become when dry; what agony they would occasion Him after the scourging and along the Way of the Cross as they rubbed against the raw wounds, when they were dragged off and on, when He fell; what He will suffer when they are torn from Him now. He has come to His death in a state too horrible for description, yet not piteous enough to arouse compassion in the thousands that have come to see Him die.

The executioners order Him to lie down upon the cross that they may take the measure for the nails. This done, they thrust Him aside whilst they bore the holes in the wood. See Him pushed here and there, not knowing where to stand in His misery, as closer and closer, driven forward by the multitude pressing up the slope, crowds the coarse, cruel rabble. It is with difficulty the centurion and his band keep it back, and leave the executioners room to do their work. Pity our Lord. Try to realise what He suffers. Wonder how His love could go so far; how the reverence due to His Majesty did not compel Him to forego ignominy such as this!

All is ready. The condemned are called for. Each lays himself down upon his cross, the thieves blaspheming in their despair, our Lord praying. The terror of His human Soul is beyond words. No martyr, no criminal ever quailed like this before torture and death. For He knows all that is to come. Every pang from now to the death struggle is vividly present to Him. He does not divert His mind from it. He does not seek to repulse the horror it produces. He allows it to assail Him with the most vehement repugnance. And He overcomes all with the love that will love us even unto death. Compassionate Him in this strife between the inferior part of the Soul that shrinks from torments and death, and the superior which rules that at such exceeding cost we shall be redeemed. From this strife we learn that repugnance which is conquered by the energy of the will, far from lessening enhances the heroism of love.

Our Lord lies down upon His cross and stretches out His arms. An executioner holds His right hand. Another takes a four-sided nail about three inches long, and with one strong blow drives it through the palm into the wood. A convulsive shudder runs through the whole frame; the limbs contract;

the knees are drawn up. The left hand will not reach the hole on the other side. They draw a noose round the wrist and stretch the arm till the sinews give way and the joints are dislocated. At last they bring it to its place, and a blow nails it fast. By means of ropes the feet are drawn to the holes in the stem of the cross and nailed there. Then the executioners rise and survey their work.

How different is the live crucifix from the white figure, unscathed except for the wounds in hands and feet, that we behold so often and so heedlessly! The Form hung aloft on Calvary is a sight almost too fearful to look upon. One alone of the many tortures inflicted on It was sufficient to cause death. The scourging, the thorny crown, the thirst, would have killed the strongest man. This Man is the most exquisitely fashioned of the children of men: His Body the most delicate, His Soul the most sensitive. How, then, can He endure so much? Because His Divinity supports Him, not for the mitigation but for the prolongation of His pain. It sustains the physical frame that it may suffer beyond the limit of natural endurance. But It hides Itself from the Soul that He may sorrow as no other has ever sorrowed: "He treadeth the winepress of the fierceness of the wrath of God, the Almighty" (Apoc. 19). "I have trodden the winepress alone" (Isaias 63).

Besides the agony in hands and feet, and the dislocation of the bones, there is the torture suffered on or near the surface of the body, where physicians say pain is most intense by reason of the nerves that are there. These nerves through the rending of the flesh in the scourging, are exposed, and the pain caused by dragging the limbs to and fro over the rough wood has been excruciating.

The crosses are raised into position; dropped into their sockets and made firm by wedges driven in with heavy blows. The dislocated limbs have to bear the shock and the torture of these blows and of those by which the title of the cross is nailed above His head. The whole weight of the disjointed frame is now borne by the wounded hands and feet. The head falls forward, unable in its agony to hold itself erect. The eyes see, dimly through the darkness that has fallen on the earth, a vast throng pouring through the Judgment Gate and massing itself round Calvary; every face turned towards Him, some few in pity, almost all in hate. He sees into every soul there. He knows what He has done for each, what He is doing now for each. He offers His torments and His death, not only for all before Him there, but for every soul that has been created and that is to be created to the end of time.

Pushing their way through the people, come a crowd of priests, scribes, and ancients. They stand triumphant before the cross to mock Him in His misery: "Vah! thou that destroyest the Temple of God and in three days dost rebuild it, save thy own self. If thou be the Son of God, come down from the cross…He saved others, Himself He cannot save. Let Christ the King of Israel come down now from the cross that we may see and believe." The soldiers mock Him, offering Him vinegar and saying: "If thou be the King of the Jews, save thyself." One of the robbers blaspheming says: "If thou be Christ, save thyself and us." Priests, soldiers, thieves all taunting Him with His Helplessness; all defying Him; all uniting in the cry: "Come down from the cross!"

The darkness deepens. With it comes fear over the souls of men. The scoffers are silent. "And all the multitude of them that were come together to that sight, and saw the things that were done, returned striking their breasts." Now at last there is room for the Mother by the side of her Son. John leads her to the foot of the cross. Magdalen, heart broken, falls down before it. The Beloved disciple looks up into His face on whose breast he leaned at supper last night.

The hours drag slowly on. Three hours the Son hangs in torture, His limbs trembling, His wounds smarting in the chill March air. Three hours His Mother stands beside Him—erect, not swooning, not turning her eyes or her mind from the contemplation of the Victim hanging there, with whose bloody Sacrifice she unites the agony of her bleeding heart. She stands: her delicate, sensitive frame strung up to that endurance. She stands: unfaltering in her oblation, whilst Simeon's sword makes its way deeper and deeper into her soul. No weakness, no lamentation: "*Ecce ancilla!*" as in the quiet midnight at Nazareth. It is the Father's Will: "Behold the handmaid of the Lord!"

The end draws on. During the three hours the body has been continually sinking, widening the wounds till it seems as if the hands must give way and it will be torn from the nails. The words that have come painfully at intervals have ceased. The breathing becomes more and more laboured. The head droops lower on the breast. The eyes get glazed and fixed. A grey shadow settles on the face. There are two gasping sobs—the next, surely, must be the last. Suddenly, the head lifts; the lips part. A loud cry goes out over the Mount and is carried far into the distance: "Father, into Thy hands I commend My spirit!" The head drops on the breast. The Heart is still. The Soul is with the Father. He has been obedient unto death, even the death of the cross. He has loved us to the end.

> Was Jesus comforted that hour
> By thought of me;
> Counting my love a meet return
> For Calvary?
>
> Or was it my ingratitude
> These many years
> That filled His Heart with agony
> His eyes with tears?

III. Father, forgive them, for they know not what they do.—Luke xxiii.

Mark the time and the place of this prayer.

Our Lord is lying on the cross. His right hand has been nailed. The left is being violently dragged to its place. The sinews give way under the strain. The joints are dislocated. At last it is stretched to the hole, and with heavy strokes of the hammer the second nail is driven in. The whole body writhes in agony. The knees are drawn up; the eyes close; the brow contracts with the intensity of the torture. Now is the moment of His prayer. He begins at once His work of Mediator; begins as men are nailing Him to the cross, to secure their pardon: "Father, forgive them for they know not what they do." Is not the self-forgetfulness of our Blessed Lord almost beyond belief! Would not His charity prove Him to be divine were all other evidence wanting!

The Jews had seen Him give sight to the blind, cleanse the lepers, free the possessed, cure every disease and every infirmity, raise the dead. They had heard Him preach a sublime doctrine, silence all cavillers, speak as never man spake. He had read their thoughts, fulfilled their prophecies, proved Himself their long-expected Messiah. And they had hated and rejected Him. They had shut their eyes to His miracles, and their ears to His invitations and His warnings.

They had stirred up His people against Him, delivered Him to the Gentiles to be put to death, and invoked His Blood in condemnation upon themselves and upon their children. How could He find excuse for them? How could He plead their ignorance?

O tender and forgiving Lord! Who will fear Thy condemnation after this? Who will fear Thee even as Judge, provided we do not refuse the pardon for which Thou pleadest so earnestly! Can I mistrust Thee, or doubt Thy most earnest desire to save me? Will not the charity that made Thee defend Thy crucifiers help Thee to find excuse, too, for me? Indeed I did not know what I was doing when I sinned against Thee. I do not understand even now the hatefulness and ingratitude of sin. It does not fill me with horror for I am blind. I fall into it easily for I am weak. Plead for me, dear Lord, with the Father that I may be forgiven for the past, and so enlighten and strengthen me that I may be kept from sin for the time to come.

"*They know not what they do.*" How different are my harsh judgments and my vindictiveness from the charity of my Saviour. How hard I find it to make excuses for those who injure or annoy me. Do I even attempt to make any? Have I not a habit of taking the severest view of an action which will bear an unfavourable interpretation? And of justifying my severity on the ground that I cannot shut my eyes to the truth? What should I have said on Calvary? Could I have found a single pretext for extenuating the sin of the Jews? Yet the Eternal Truth excused them and pleaded for them.

O meek and loving Lord, make my heart like unto Thine, patient, kind, thinking no evil, bearing all things, believing all things, hoping all things, enduring all things!

"*Father, forgive them!*" Offer this tender prayer, Lord, for all near and dear to me who stand in need of Thy special mercy; for all who at this hour are crucifying again the Son of God (Heb. 6). In Thy prayer is my trust. "For if any man sin we have an Advocate with the Father, Jesus Christ the just. And He is the propitiation for our sins, and not for ours only but also for those of the whole world" (I. John, 2). Wherefore, "O God, our Protector, look on the face of Thy Christ" (Ps. 83). Hear His prayer for all sinners. Be infinitely merciful in Thy judgments of us all. "Thou sparest all because they are Thine, Lord who lovest souls" (Wisd. 11). "For if we sin we are Thine" (Wisd. 15). Frail children, yet Thy children still. Recall us to Thyself by the grace of contrition. Receive us for His sake who gave Himself for us. And grant us that forgiveness for which He prayed.

> IV. And he said to Jesus: Lord, remember me when Thou shalt come into Thy Kingdom.
>
> And Jesus said to him: Amen, I say to thee this day thou shalt be with Me in Paradise.—Luke xxiii.

What is there kingly about Him as He hangs on His cross between the thieves? He lies under the same condemnation with them. He is placed in the midst as the most guilty. He has been followed to the place of execution with a vehemence of hatred which they have been spared. Above His head is His cause written: "King of the Jews." But it is nailed there in derision. Covered with wounds and bruises, defiled with spittle, the reproach of men and the outcast of the people, what is there to proclaim Him King?

Look at the poor thieves, His companions. They are suffering sorely. Yet something yonder is riveting the attention of one, and stirring his soul to its depths. In that fellow-sufferer on his left, that Man tortured almost out of the likeness of man, he discerns a majesty that neither pain nor indignity can disturb. He sees Him looking down with gentleness on the rabble that are feasting their eyes on His agony. From the parched lips he hears no word of indignation or complaint; but again and again, broken by the sobs of the death struggle: "Father forgive them." He looks, He listens. He ponders. Grace comes and is not rejected. Faith shows him in this outcast the King of Kings. Hope that was dead an hour ago revives. Love draws him strangely to this Friend found so late. For the robber feels He is not a King only, but a Friend. He has not spoken, but His eyes have turned this way more than once, and whilst that look rested on him all pain was forgotten. Who can it be that has power to draw his soul like this? Oh that he could fling himself at His feet; that he might belong to Him; that he might be with Him in that life on which they are entering as he is with Him now; that he might not be altogether forgotten by Him whose presence is soothing his last hour! A passionate desire wakes within his soul to reveal itself, to cast itself on the mercy of Him who hangs there. But will this Holy One spurn him? Will his King reject him? He flings away the thought. He gives no heed to the reviling of his fellow-robber; no heed to the fury he will provoke down there. A cry goes forth: "Lord, remember me when Thou shalt come into Thy Kingdom!"

And see! The thorn-crowned head that lay drooping on the breast is lifted. It turns to him. The eyes dulling with the mist of death, painfully raise themselves to his. The dry lips open, and words come thick and slow: "Amen—I say—to thee—this day thou shalt—be with Me—in Paradise."

A remembrance was all the thief had asked. The answer was pardon for the sins of a life, final perseverance, canonisation while living, the promise of heaven, and—happiest of all—reunion with his Master before the sun had set. Can we trust our Lord to be tender and generous with us when we return to Him? Does not His royal Heart proclaim Him King!

Remember me! The thief had but a short space for prayer. He had much to pray for. In two words he prayed, and his prayer covered all his needs.

I, too, have but a short time for prayer. Life will soon be done, the little space wherein I am to obtain from God all I want for my eternal happiness. And I, like the thief, may be content with the cry that includes every petition: "Lord, remember me!"

Remember me in my present necessities, in the actual state of my soul as it is in Thy sight. Remember its wounds and its weakness, the result of sin in the past. Remember its trials, its temptations, its weariness. Remember the peculiar difficulties and dangers consequent on temperament, early influences, circumstances, and the way my will has borne itself towards all these things.

Remember, O Lord, the love with which from eternity Thou hast brooded over my soul; with which Thou didst create, and redeem, and sanctify it. Remember Thine ideal in creating it, and the graces Thou hast prepared for it with a view to that ideal. Remember that "the gifts and the calling of God are without repentance" (Rom. 11); that Thy love and Thy purpose remain firm in spite of the waywardness by which I have crossed Thy designs. That I may not disappoint Thee, may not waste what Thou hast lavished on me, or lessen by any shortcoming on my part the glory Thou hast put it in my power to render Thee—for Thine own sake, therefore, my God,—remember me.

Remember my desires—those aspirations after better things that are the fruit of Thy grace; that subsist in spite of all my inconsistencies and failings.

Remember my responsibilities—the dread influence which, whether I will or no, I exercise on those about me, those especially who are dependent on me.

Remember me, O Lord, when the figure of this world is passing away, when we shall see Thee coming in glory to judge the living and the dead. Remember me when Thou shalt come into Thy Kingdom, that where Thou art I too may be.

Remember me in life, remember me in death; in time and in eternity, O Lord, remember me!

> V. When Jesus therefore had seen His Mother and the disciple standing whom He loved, He saith to His Mother: Woman, behold thy son.
>
> After that He saith to the disciple: Behold thy Mother.
> And from that hour the disciple took her to his own.

She was His last gift kept for the end. He had declared His Father to be ours: "I ascend to My Father and to your Father" (John 20). He had promised us His Holy Spirit: "If I go I will send Him to you" (John 16). He had given us Himself; "This is My Body…This is My Blood" (Matth. 26). He had parted for our sakes with all He had in this world—His followers, His friends, His fame, His honour. What was left to Him? She to whom He came at first, His Mother. He will give her away now. We must not be able to say there is anything, however dear to Him, however specially His own, that He has not shared with us. He must prove His right to the title of our Elder Brother by making His Mother the Mother of us all. As He has said: "My Father and your Father," He will say: "My Mother and yours." Heartbroken, she was standing beneath His cross by the disciple whom He loved. Jesus saith to her: "Woman, behold thy son." After that He saith to the disciple: "Behold thy Mother."

"And from that hour the disciple took her to his own." He took her to sanctify the home at Ephesus and Jerusalem as with her Divine Son she had sanctified the home at Nazareth. It is the mother that makes the home. It is her influence that pervades it and determines its spirit. She is its brightness and its joy, the common possession and resource, the comforter, the peacemaker, the provider, the counsellor. The Mother of God is given to Christian homes to be all this to them. But the gift must be accepted. John received with reverence, gratitude, and love the treasure bequeathed to him. We must do the like.

O Mother of Jesus be to me what thou wert to the beloved Disciple. Be to my home what thou wert to his. Like John I receive thee as a precious gift to me and mine. Like him I promise thee the honour, love, and trust of a child. Like him I take thee to my own.

VI. My God, My God, why hast Thou forsaken Me?—Mark xv.

Our Lord loves to call Himself "the Son of Man," and there is none among His many titles to which He has more fully proved His claim. He came to us in His Incarnation resolved to share with us all He could share. He would come down to our level. He would know by experience our trials and our sorrows. In the execution of His design there were difficulties all but insuperable. But the Omnipotence of His Love overcame them. We are wayfarers, journeying painfully

The Crucifixion

to our Country, to the Vision of God there which will satisfy every desire. His Soul enjoyed the Beatific Vision from the moment of Its creation. And that Vision is incompatible with pain. But His Almighty Power could suspend Its effects. He suspended them. Now He could suffer with us cold, heat, hunger, weariness. Sickness He could not suffer. But He would more than compensate for this by the torments of His Passion. "From the sole of the foot to the top of the head there should be no soundness in Him, wounds and bruises, and swelling sores" (Isaias 1). Whilst we employ anaesthetics, and ask for miracles to avert suffering, He will use His Omnipotence to bring it within His reach. Thus will He be at one and the same time with us on the way to cheer and support, and at the term to reward us.

But there was a deeper depth yet to which He must descend if He would be like us in all things. Sin has fixed a gulf between us and our God. It has hidden His face from us, and then left us wailing in our despair. Here surely the Son of Man must part company with us, He "who did no sin neither was guile found in his mouth" (1 Peter 2). No, for He is come to seek and to save that which was lost. He will follow us down into our misery that He may rescue us. Sin cannot touch Him. But its chastisement He can draw down upon Himself. He has undertaken to satisfy for us to the full, to bear all that He may bear consistently with the dignity of His Person. Therefore He will endure as far as possible the most awful form of human suffering—separation from God, dereliction by God.

"When the sixth hour was come there was darkness over the whole earth until the ninth hour" (Mark 15). And there was darkness deeper and more terrible over the human Soul of Jesus. Among His unspeakable sufferings the keenest was this hiding of the face of the Father. We have no thoughts or images whereby to bring home to ourselves in the very least the love with which the Soul of Christ turned to the Father. "I and the Father are one" (John 10). "As the Father knoweth Me, and I know the Father" (Id). "I live by the Father" (John 6). To be about His Father's business He had come into the world. That His Father's Name might be hallowed He had taught, and toiled, and suffered. It was when He spoke of the Father that His full Heart revealed Itself. To the Father's face He lifted His eyes, weary with the sin and sorrow of earth. The Father's bosom was rest when heavy at heart He lay in prayer on the mountain side by night. The Father's love was His all-sufficing compensation for the coldness and ingratitude of men.

And now the Father's face was turned away from Him. The chastisement of our sins was upon Him. The loneliness, helplessness, terror that the sense of estrangement from God brings upon the soul, He allowed Himself to feel for our sakes. Can He descend lower than this? Is He not now at last like to us in all things?

VII. I thirst. John xix.

God's way is to reward, to punish, to satisfy for sin, in kind. The working of this law we see throughout the Passion. To make reparation for our misuse of the senses our Lord suffers from the sole of the foot to the crown of the head. His thirst on the cross is an atonement for the sin that lost Paradise and occasions the loss daily of so many souls.

"*I thirst.*" Nothing causes thirst like loss of blood. Think of all He had lost since the Agony on Thursday night. The abundance of His sweat in the Garden is shown by the words, "trickling down upon the ground." Therefore it had first soaked His garments. The scourging left the body one raw wound. The bleeding of His head pierced with the thorns was a still further drain. A terrible thirst was upon Him when He came to His Crucifixion. They offered Him the drink provided for the condemned, wine mingled with a stupifying substance to deaden somewhat the sufferer's pangs. "And when He had tasted He would not drink" (Matth. 27). He refused the draught because He would admit of no relief. He tasted the gall that the only sense in Him which had escaped torment might pay the penalty due to our sinful indulgence of the taste.

"*I thirst.*" We are told that crucifixion is one of the most awful forms of death the cruelty of man has devised. And that among its tortures the most intolerable is thirst. In itself this is sufficient to cause death. We know what our Lord could bear in silence. Yet even He exclaimed: "I thirst." It was not a complaint. He suffered too willingly for that. It was a revelation of the extremity of His pain. And it was a warning. He would let us know something of what our self-indulgence was costing Him; of what the sin of intemperance deserves. Hoarsely the words came from the parched throat. He could scarcely speak. The tongue was cleaving to the palate. Think what His Mother felt as she looked up and saw His agony and was powerless to help Him.

Happy the man who—we may hope in pity—raised the sponge of vinegar and water to His lips to give Him some slight relief! Have I no desire to give Him any? Can I watch Him in His torments and be content with a little barren compassion? Can I find it in my heart to leave Him to suffer quite alone? O my Lord let me bear Thee company by a little voluntary penance. By some privation, trifling it may be but constant, let me prove my gratitude for the burning thirst Thou hast endured for me!

    VIII. Father, into Thy hands I commend My spirit.—Luke xxiii.

Had we been told that our God was coming to live with us on earth to teach us the way to heaven, could we have dreamed that He would show us by His own example how to die? Yet this is the lesson of all others it behoves us to learn. Death is the all-important act that cannot be practised or repeated, and on the right performance of which the first time eternity depends.

Would it have been like Him, then, to leave us untaught? Or to leave the task of teaching us to any other? No. Therefore He calls us all round the Cross to see Him die. He will show us by His own words and example what is the safest, the most perfect disposition in which we can render up our souls to God. Let us listen:

"*Father, into Thy hands I commend My spirit.*" A while ago it was the piteous cry to the Creator: "My God, My God, why hast Thou forsaken me?" Now it is the filial commendation to the Father. The lesson He wants us to have ready for our last hour is confidence. Had there been any other better He would have taught it. We must learn it now. We ought to be perpetually rehearsing for the hour of our death, as the Church teaches us in the Hail Mary. And the most important thing to rehearse is confidence. Again and again the trusting commendation now, that it may come helpfully to our lips then: "Father, into Thy hands I commend my spirit."

Father—my Father, "who hast loved me with an everlasting love, and drawn me taking pity on me" (Jer. 31), "who hast made me and created me" (Deut. 22), and "called me by my name" (Isaias 45), remember that it is not as Maker and Creator but as Father that Thy Son has taught us to speak to Thee: "Our Father who art in heaven."

I am a prodigal; I have wasted my substance. I am not worthy to be called Thy child. But Thou art my Father still, merciful, long-suffering, and full of compassion (2 Esdras 9). "For if we sin we are Thine" (Wisd. 15).

O my Father, when life on earth is ending, take me to the Home where Thou art awaiting me, Thy House with its many mansions where Thou hast prepared my place. Take me to Thyself who alone canst satisfy me: "for what have I in heaven besides Thee!" (Ps. 72).

Into Thy hands—the hands that have formed me and guided me, provided for me, shielded me, blessed me, sustained me to the end:

I commend—with a child's unquestioning trust—

My spirit—my one possession in the hour of my death, all that will remain to me of what I have in this world. As it goes forth from the body, alone and trembling, assailed by enemies, beyond the reach of friends, receive it, O Father, into Thy hands. Have pity on it because it is my only one. "Let not the enemy prevail against it, nor the son of iniquity have power to hurt it" (Ps. 88). "To the work of Thy hands stretch out Thy right hand" (Job 14). In union with my dying Saviour I confide it to Thy mercy now for the hour of my death: Father, into Thy hands I commend my spirit.

IX. Come down from the Cross!—Mark xv.

"Come down from the cross!" is like that other taunt in the desert: "If Thou be the Son of God, cast Thyself down"

(Luke 4). The challenge was given, not on Calvary only or in the wilderness. Not to Him alone who he suspected might be the Son of God by nature, but to the adopted children of God also, the enemy cries out: "Cast thyself down."

There is nothing the devil fears like perseverance in well doing. He can put up with spasmodic piety, with good works zealously *begun*. What he dreads is the courage that holds out under difficulties, that perseveres to the end. "Come down from the cross," he says to us.

What is our cross? All that goes against self. All that it costs to reduce self; to act on principle; to submit to authority; to accommodate ourselves to others; to be faithful to irksome duties; to struggle against self-indulgence and the softness of our times; to be energetic in attention to our weak point; to bear up against failure and the monotony of daily routine; to be resigned when all seems to go wrong. Whatever goes counter to our liking, in our circumstances, our health, our companions, the way things are done, the way things turn out—all this is our cross.

And our enemy says: "Come down from the cross." Why so much self restraint? Take things easily: violence never lasts. Do as others do, as So-and-so, a good person does. Have a good time whilst you can.

We, like our Master, have to turn a deaf ear to the tempter, to hold out to the end, to persevere on our cross as long as God wills; battling with suffering, battling with self, often by that hardest form of conflict—endurance. The hour of rest will come for us as it came for Him. After the temptation in the desert "the devil left Him, and behold Angels came and ministered to Him" (Matth. 4). After the final contest with the Evil One on Calvary, "Christ dieth no more, death shall no more have dominion over Him" (Rom. 6). But until God's hour came for the cessation of the struggle, He persevered on His cross. He was taken down by the Father's Will when the time was come.

X. So he became their Saviour…in His love and in His mercy He redeemed them.—Isaias lxiii.

(1) God so loved the world as to give His Only-begotten Son that whosoever believeth in Him may not perish but may have everlasting life (John 3).

(2) If thou didst know the gift of God! (John 4).

(3) You were not redeemed with corruptible things, as gold and silver, but with the precious Blood of Christ (1 Pet. 1).

(4) You are not your own for you are bought with a great price (1 Cor. 6).

(5) Christ hath loved us and hath delivered Himself for us (Ephes. 5).

(6) Loved us and washed us from our sins in His own Blood (Apoc. 1).

(7) Loved me and delivered Himself for me (Galat. 2).

(8) Who, then, shall separate us from the love of Christ? (Rom. 8).

(9) The Lamb that was slain is worthy to receive power, and divinity, and wisdom, and strength, and honour, and glory, and benediction (Apoc. 5).

(10) If any man love not our Lord Jesus Christ, let him be anathema (1 Cor. 16).

III. The Glorious Mysteries

The Resurrection

I. This is the day which the Lord hath made: let us be glad and rejoice therein.—Ps. cxvii.

AND in the end of the Sabbath, when it began to dawn towards the first day of the week, came Mary Magdalen and Salome to the sepulchre, the sun being now risen. And they said one to another: "Who shall roll us back the stone from the door of the sepulchre?" And looking, they saw the stone rolled back. For it was very great.

She (Magdalen) ran, therefore, and cometh to Simon Peter, and to the other disciple whom Jesus loved, and saith to them: "They have taken away the Lord out of the sepulchre, and we know not where they have laid Him."

And entering into the sepulchre, they (the other two women, Mary of James, and Salome) saw a young man sitting at the right side clothed with a white robe, and they were astonished. Who said to them: "Be not affrighted, you seek Jesus of Nazareth, who was crucified. He is not here, for He is risen as He said. Come and see the place where the Lord was laid. And going quickly tell His disciples and Peter that He is risen. And behold, He will go before you into Galilee. There you shall see Him as He told you. Lo! I have foretold it to you." But they going out fled from the sepulchre; for a trembling and fear had seized them; and they said nothing to any man, for they were afraid. And they went…quickly… with fear and great joy, running to tell His disciples.

But Mary stood at the sepulchre without, weeping. Now as she was weeping, she stooped down, and looked into the sepulchre. And she saw two angels in white, sitting, one at the head, and one at the feet, where the body of Jesus had been laid. They say to her: "Woman, why weepest thou?" She saith to them: "Because they have taken away my Lord, and I know not where they have laid Him."

When she had thus said, she turned herself back, and saw Jesus standing; and she knew not that it was Jesus. Jesus saith unto her: "Woman, why weepest thou? whom seekest thou?" She thinking that it was the gardener, saith to Him: "Sir, if thou hast taken Him hence, tell me where thou hast laid Him; and I will take Him away."

Jesus saith to her: "Mary." She turning, saith to Him: "*Rabboni*," (which is to say: Master).

And behold Jesus met them (the other two women), saying: "All hail." But they came up, and took hold of His feet, and adored Him. Then Jesus said to them: "Fear not.

Go, tell My brethren that they go into Galilee, there they shall see Me."

And it was Mary Magdalen, and Joanna and Mary of James and the other two women that were with them, who told these things to the Apostles. And these words seemed to them as idle tales; and they did not believe them.

Now when it was late that same day, the first of the week, and the doors were shut, where the disciples were gathered together for fear of the Jews, Jesus came and stood in the midst, and said to them: "Peace be to you, it is I, fear not." But they being troubled and frighted, supposed that they saw a spirit.

And He said to them: "Why are you troubled, and why do thoughts arise in your hearts? See My hands and feet, that it is I Myself; handle, and see; for a spirit hath not flesh and bones, as you see Me to have." And when He had said this, He shewed them His hands and feet, and His side. The disciples therefore were glad, when they saw the Lord (Matth. 28, Mark 16, Luke 24, John 20).

See the Soul of Christ passing swift as light from the mangled Body on the Cross to the Limbo of the Fathers. See the vast sombre region lit up at its entrance as with a thousand suns. Behold how by one impulse its eager millions are borne towards Him and fall prostrate in adoration—Adam and Eve; David and Isaias, the Prophets of the Incarnation; the Gentile Job; St. Joseph; the holy Baptist.

Hear the acclamations, the praise, the thanksgiving.

Taste the jubilee of that hour in Limbo when up above on the frightened earth all was darkness and desolation. Notice that this difference is due to one cause only—the Presence of Christ.

II. Free among the dead.—Ps. lxxxvii.

We speak of helplessness during life, but what is it to our utter helplessness after death! Think of it. The body carried anywhere, treated in any way, delivered over to the dishonour of the grave. The soul, free a moment ago to choose its course, fixed now in its eternal state; presented at the Judgment seat for sentence, and taken instantly to the place where the sentence is to be carried out. If to the prison-house of Hell or Purgatory, what helplessness for it there! Yes, truly, our helplessness after death is absolute.

Not thus was it with our Head. A moment before death He was "as a man without help" (Ps. 87). Hands and feet nailed, every limb, every nerve without help in their intolerable pain: His mighty Soul, crushed under the weight of the Father's anger, summing up Its anguish in the cry: "My God, My God, why hast Thou forsaken Me?"

After death—the moment after—what a change! The body, lifeless, it is true, but embalmed with the Divinity, awaiting in a three days rest the instant of its glorious Resurrection: "In peace, in the selfsame I will sleep and I will rest" (Ps. 4). The Soul—oh what a change for It! "Free among the dead" (Ps. 87). Free, absolutely free, free as It had never been before. The suffering that had weighed upon It from the moment of the Incarnation—gone! The ever-present sight of Calvary—gone! The burden of the sins of men—gone! The cloud that hid the face of the Father—gone! The very possibility of pain—gone from It for ever!

O my Lord, this is the thought that fills my soul with such overflowing gladness—that Thy blessed Human Soul is free at last. What must have been the weight that lay upon

It always during the three and thirty years! Always, always. When It prayed and laboured. When taking in all sin and sorrow, past, present, and to come, It suffered the pain of this knowledge to coexist with the bliss of the Beatific Vision. Above all, when It bore the hiding of the Father's Face during the Passion! O well-beloved Son, begotten of the Father from eternity, what must have been the torture of separation from Him with whom Thou hast but one undivided Nature: what the relief the instant after death, that that pain was passed away for ever.

"Free among the dead." This is the glad thought that fills my soul with peace and joy as the clock strikes three on Good Friday; that is quiet jubilee all through the hours of Saturday; that leaps up in exultation at sunrise on Easter Day. Free! Free! Free! It was the cry of Mary's heart when in Thy risen beauty Thou didst stand before her. She looked at eyes, and hands, and feet—free! The smile for the first time was free. In Bethlehem, in Nazareth, when Thou camest to her at intervals during the Public Life, Thy smile was always the sunshine of her soul. Yet there was that about it which told of the hidden burden of the Man of Sorrows. On Easter morning that smile was free, and she drank in its new beauty with the adoration of the creature and the overflowing joy of the Mother's heart.

I adore and rejoice with her. O my Risen Lord, I can say nothing, think of nothing yet but this: "Free! Free! I will rejoice presently with Thy friends to whom Thou bearest Thine own joy. I will see Thee freeing them from doubt, and fear, and sorrow. I will ask Thee to free me from all that stands between my soul and Thee. But now for a little while let me kneel before Thee—quite alone. Let me pour out my heart to Thee who readest it through and through, and knowest all it would say, and wilt count as faith, and love, and adoration, and praise, its cry of Easter joy—"Free! Free!"

III. Hail! full of grace, the Lord is with thee.—Luke i.

She is alone. All day she has been the refuge of the scattered flock. One by one they have made their way to her, Peter, and James, and Magdalen, and Salome. They could not share her faith and her hope, but her presence soothed them in their wretchedness. Instinctively they turned to her. Into her ear they poured their bitter sorrow. The sympathy of her motherly heart kept their hearts from hardening into despair. Yet their tears flowed faster as they looked into her face. She was all they had now; all that remained to them of Him. And she was so like Him. Her voice had His tones in it. Her ways were like His. Her counsel reminded them of Him. Even thus He would have said. So He used to comfort them when they came to Him in trouble. Yes, they must keep near her. Shared with her, their anguish was less intolerable, and, somehow, almost seemed less hopeless.

Thus, in the darkness of her own desolation, our Mother began her appointed task. She was Comforter of the afflicted, "giving to all abundantly and upbraiding not," all that sad Saturday.

And now night has come and she is alone. Even Magdalen has left her side. There is still something that faithful heart may do for Him. The spices are bought, but there are preparations to be made for the early visit to the Sepulchre on the morrow.

The Mother of Sorrows is alone. Yes, alone. He must have her all to Himself when He comes. Not even Gabriel here, as in the first coming to Nazareth; unless, indeed, as her Guardian Angel, he is privileged to be near her even now.

The sweetest and tenderest of our Lord's visits on Easter Day, those in which He had wounds to heal deeper even than His dear Magdalen's, are shrouded in secrecy till the day when the secrets of all hearts shall be revealed. Of the interview with Peter we are told nothing beyond the fact. Of the interview with His Mother, what need to tell even the fact! What heart that believes He came to the world by her, that she stood by Him to the end, has to be told on the word of God, that He came to her first in His risen life!

She is alone—stricken as no creature has ever been, as no other mother could have been, and lived. She has borne with Him all they undertook to bear together for our sakes, when she said at Nazareth: *"Ecce ancilla!"* She has lived it through, but the frail vessel is all but shattered. His Presence alone can revive the spirit that is pining for Him; His Voice alone recall to it joy and gladness; His Hand draw the sword from out that broken heart. "For He woundeth and cureth, He striketh, and His Hands shall heal" (Job 5).

The night wears on. Again and again her eye turns to the window that looks east. No streaks of light as yet. She waits in silence and in hope, the handmaid of the Lord, hastening by her desires His second coming into the world in His Risen life, as, we are told, she had accelerated the hour of the Incarnation: "God, my God, for Thee do I watch at break of day. For Thee my soul hath thirsted; for Thee my flesh, how many ways!" (Ps. 62.) "As the hart panteth after the fountains of water, so panteth my soul after Thee, God! My soul hath thirsted after the living God...My tears

The Resurrection

have been my bread day and night, whilst it is said to me daily: Where is thy God?" (Ps. 41.)

Wait, blessed mourner, wait! Light is breaking in the east. It begins to dawn towards the first day of the week. Yet a few moments and "thy Light shall come, and the glory of the Lord shall rise upon thee" (Isaias 60). A few moments and "the Lord God shall wipe away all tears from thy eyes" (Apoc. 21). "If He delay, wait for Him, for He will surely come and will not be slack" (Hab. 2).

"Sing praise and rejoice, O daughter of Sion! for behold I come" (Zach. 2). "I am risen, and am still with thee."

See her! One moment in desolation worse than death. The next, at His feet, in His embrace who is "the breath of her mouth, Christ the Lord" (Lament. 4). She has fallen at His feet, for He is God. He has folded her in His arms, for He is her Son.

O Son of Mary, was there ever joy on earth like the joy of Thy Heart when Thou didst meet Thy Virgin Mother, and fold her in that Easter embrace, and according to the multitude of the sorrows of her heart make her glad with Thy consolation?

Were ever tears so blissful, Mother, as those which were wiped away by the Hand of thy Son and thy God in that first hour of the Resurrection? Look, blessed one, through those tears of joy and see that it is He Himself. Look upon that face, the face of thy Christ. Look upon the face on which the Angels desire to look; thy right is before every other. Look with thy adoration and thy love. Worship for us what for us was buffeted, and bruised, and dishonoured. Worship it with thy praise and thy thanksgiving, with the humility of His handmaid, with, the pride of Thy Mother's heart. See with delight how the dazzling glory of that face leaves uneclipsed the human beauty of the three and thirty years. O blessed among women, blessed by all generations, enter into the joy of thy Lord; share in the triumph of thy Son!

"The winter is now past, the rain is over and gone." Hail! full of grace, the Lord is with thee.

IV. Jesus saith to her: "Mary." She turning, saith to Him: "*Rabboni.*"—John xx.

How faithful the holy women were to our Lord from the time they attached themselves to Him! They followed Him about during His preaching, ministering to Him of their substance, unmindful of private interests and social distinctions when there was question of His service. Salome and "Mary of James" gave up their sons to Him, Joanna, the wife of Herod's steward, and Magdalen, made themselves the associates and helpmates of the wives of fishermen.

But faithful among the faithful was Mary Magdalen; the most zealous, the most devoted, their recognised leader, as Peter among the Twelve. During the forty hours from the Crucifixion to the Resurrection, we find her now with one party, now with another, so prominent, that in the records of the Evangelists she stands at times for her whole company. With Mary of Cleophas at the foot of the Cross, beside the sinless Mary. When all was over on Friday evening sitting "with Mary mother of Joseph over against the sepulchre." "In the end of the Sabbath coming with Mary the mother of James to see the sepulchre." And when the Sabbath was past, going with Salome "to buy sweet spices that coming they might anoint Jesus."

"On the first day of the week Mary Magdalen cometh early when it was yet dark unto the sepulchre." A little later Mary stood at the sepulchre without weeping." The Angel had announced the glad news of the Resurrection, and her companions had gone quickly with fear and great joy running to tell His disciples. But Magdalen stands riveted to the spot where she had last seen Him, too bewildered by her grief to take in the purport of the Angel's message. Again and again she stoops down and looks into the tomb, searching still through her tears, lest by any oversight she might have missed Him. Two Angels appear, sitting, one at the head, one at the foot, where the body of Jesus had been laid. They say to her: "Woman, why weepest thou?" She saith to them: "Because they have taken away my Lord, and I know not where they have laid Him." When her companions "entering into the sepulchre, saw a young man sitting at the right side clothed with a white robe, they were astonished." Magdalen shows no surprise. She answers the Angels as if they were persons whom she might have expected to find there. Their "shining apparel" does not distract her from her grief: "They have taken away my Lord, and I know not where they have laid Him."

How could He whom she sought so perseveringly fail to show Himself to her? His first appearances were for those who had been faithful to Him unto death. His Blessed Mother, Mary Magdalen, the holy women. His Mother has seen Him. Magdalen is to see Him now.

A sound attracts her attention. She turns her tearful face to the mouth of the cave and sees One standing there whom she knows not. Repeating the Angels words, He says to her: "Woman, why weepest thou? Whom seekest thou?"

"Why weepest thou?" There is no chiding in those tones of pitying tenderness. Presently on the road to Emmaus He will rebuke two downcast disciples: "O foolish and slow of heart, to believe in all things which the prophets have spoken." Later on He will upbraid the Eleven "for their incredulity and hardness of heart." Magdalen's faith and hope were at fault like theirs. But her love and her tears, as of old, stayed all upbraiding on His lips. He had reprehended Simon for his hard thoughts of her. He had chidden Martha who complained of her. But for the sinner out of whom He had cast seven devils He had never a word but of tenderest mercy. Against the Pharisee He defended her: "Many sins are forgiven her because she hath loved much." Against her sister: "Mary hath chosen the best part which shall not be taken away from her." Against His own disciples: "Let her alone. Why do you molest her?"

It was her contrite love, her loving contrition, that thus won His Heart. He had no reproach for her whose tears were her confession, and sorrow, and satisfaction. So high was she raised in grace and favour, that she had her own way with Him. She sent for Him in her trouble: "Lord, He whom Thou lovest is sick." And He came. She expostulated with Him for His delay: "Lord, if Thou hadst been here my brother had not died." And "Jesus groaned in the spirit and troubled Himself." She led Him where she would: "Lord, come and see." And "when He saw her weeping…Jesus wept."

Oh those tears of Mary's, what they obtained from Christ! Once only had He seemed unmindful of them. It was three days ago when at the foot of the Cross they fell like rain, mingling with the blood that was being shed for her. Yet He was heeding them even then. A higher grace than consolation was granted her on Calvary—the privilege of sharing in His own desolation, of tasting next after His Blessed Mother the bitterness of His chalice.

She had been made partaker of the sufferings of Christ: the hour was come for her to share His triumph and His joy.

"Whom seekest thou?" the Stranger asked. What a question for that loving heart. Thou knowest, Lord, that from the time her tears fell on Thy feet, she has sought Thee alone. She has sought Thee humbly, bravely, perseveringly. And Thou hast said: "Seek and you shall find."

Thinking she has before her the gardener who if tactfully approached may aid her in her search, she says: "Sir, if thou hast taken Him hence, tell me where thou hast laid Him, and I will take Him away."

"Him"—no name. She supposes her Lord to be the one object in every mind and heart as in her own.

"I will take Him away." "Love often knows no measure but is inflamed above all measure. Love feels no burden, values no labours, would willingly do more than it can, complains not of impossibility because it conceives that it may and can do all things" (*Imit*. III., 5).

Our Lord can hide Himself no longer. Jesus saith to her: "Mary!" He calls her by her name as He was wont to do when she sat at His feet at Bethany. The tones of that Voice are unlike those of any other—It is Himself! She turning saith to Him: "*Rabboni!*" What fulness, what intensity of love and joy are summed up in that word. What rapture is there in this first moment of recognition, in this sudden transition from the depths of desolation to joy that is heaven begun. What compensation and more than compensation for the anguish of the past is contained in those two words: "Mary!" "*Rabboni!*" It is no vision. It is not too good to be true. See hands, and feet, and side. It is Himself: "*Rabboni!* Master!" She throws herself at His feet to kiss them once again. But He has a work for her to do first: "Go to my brethren and say to them: I ascend to My Father and to your Father, to My God and to your God." Mary Magdalen went and told them that had been with Him…and telleth the disciples: "I have seen the Lord and these things He said to me."

The Church reserves her *Credo* for Masses on high festivals, and for the Feast of her Apostles and Doctors. One exception she makes, if exception it can be called. It is for "the woman that was a sinner," whose name the Son of God will have associated with His own throughout all time; whom He Himself has made Doctor, Evangelist, Apostle to the Apostles; the bearer of the gladdest tidings earth has ever heard; the first preacher of the Gospel of the Resurrection—blessed Mary Magdalen.

> V. In the evening weeping shall have place,
> and in the morning gladness.—Ps. xxix.

What an evening was that of the first Good Friday to the disciples of Christ! The Shepherd had been stricken, and the flock was scattered. Hiding, perchance, among the tombs in the gloomy valleys round about Jerusalem, or in obscure corners of the city, they gave themselves up to the utter dejection consequent on the overthrow of all their hopes.

Sights and sounds of fear were on every side. The rending of the veil of the Temple and the disclosure of the Holy of Holies had filled every heart with consternation. And men were telling how rocks had been cloven asunder, and tombs were opening, and the bodies of the saints, arising, were coming into the city and appearing to many.

Such testimony to the Divinity of their Master might surely have saved the disciples from the blank despondency which had settled upon them. But their hopelessness was proof against the voice of nature as against the voice of the prophets. All was over. All had ended in failure. The happy days with Him only made the present and the future more intolerable. What were they to do? Go back to Galilee and to their nets, and try to forget that for three years they had been the companions, the intimate friends of Jesus of Nazareth?

Such will have been their thoughts as the evening wore on. When night fell they might have been seen creeping under cover of the darkness to the Supper room on Mount Sion. There, in all probability they kept together during the following day.

What a Pasch for them! Jerusalem was trying to rejoice, striving to forget in the celebrations of the Feast the darkness of that awful noon of yesterday. But in vain. From the palaces of Pilate and Herod, and the Chief Priests, from the Temple Courts to the remotest tent pitched on the outskirts of the city, one memory was in all minds, one Name was in every mouth.

See the Eleven talking together in the Upper Chamber, humbly gathering from the holy women the last incidents on Calvary. Watch Peter's face as they tell how to John, the only one of the Twelve there, was committed the Blessed Mother. How it was to Joseph of Arimathea and Nicodemus she had to look to render the last services to her Son. See how his tears break forth again and again; how pitying and how tender John is with him.

See Mary in her desolation, brave, unshaken in her trust, resuming in her single self the faith and hope, if not the charity of the infant Church. She believes in the triumph that is at hand. But until God's hour for consolation has come, the anguish of her soul is supreme. Yet she is not self-centred. Her motherly heart goes out to the sorrowing disciples. She strives to soothe them and to reanimate their hope. And her words have at least this success that she keeps them together in their desolation.

We wonder, perhaps, that with her absolute faith in the Resurrection on the third day, our Lady's woe could have been so complete. But the Apostle tells us "We are not sufficient for ourselves." We cannot console ourselves. A comforter must be one from without. All her life through her Comforter was God alone. And He was withholding His consolation till the appointed hour. "Therefore do I weep, and my eyes run down with water, because the Comforter, the relief of my soul, is far from me" (Lament 1).

As soon as the Sabbath rest is over, Mary Magdalen, Mary the mother of James, and Salome hasten to the bazaars to buy spices wherewith to finish the embalming of the sacred body. During the evening they make their preparations, and very early on the first day of the week "when it was yet dark," they set out for the Sepulchre. They must have known of the stone that closed the entrance, and of the seal, and the guards. Yet till they were fairly on their way, no difficulty occurred to them. Love is blind, we are told. It has certainly a marvellous inability to see obstacles in its path. Even when hindrances began to force themselves on their attention, they were not dismayed. Nothing affrighted or stopped them. Neither the darkness, nor the earthquake, nor guards, nor stone, nor the fear of the Jews, which, until the coming of the Holy Ghost, paralysed the Apostles. "Who shall roll us back the stone," was the only question. "And looking, they saw the stone rolled back." It is not God's way to leave unrewarded faith and love such as theirs. The greater the obstacle the more easily it yields to love and trust.

We see their confidence again in the absence of surprise at the miracle worked for them. They took it as a matter of course that God would help them. "And entering into the Sepulchre they saw a young man sitting at the right side clothed with a white robe, and they were astonished"—for the first time. "Who said to them: 'Fear not for I know that you seek Jesus who was crucified. He is not here, for He is risen as He said. Come, and see the place where the Lord was laid. And going quickly tell His disciples and Peter that He is risen: and behold, He will go before you into Galilee; there you shall see Him. Lo! I have foretold it to you.' And they went...quickly...with fear and great joy, running to tell His disciples."

"And behold Jesus met them, saying: 'All hail.' But they came up and took hold of His feet and adored Him. Then Jesus said to them 'Fear not, go tell My brethren that they go into Galilee, there they shall see Me.'"

Oh that we could share their adoration and their joy! He is our Master as well as theirs. To each one of us it is said as we come to meditate on the Resurrection: "Enter thou into the joy of thy Lord." That we could forget ourselves for awhile, and our little interests and sorrows! That, filled with the spirit of our Mother, the Church, we could cry out with her: "Receive, we beseech Thee, O Lord, the offerings of Thy exulting Church" (Secret for Low Sunday). "This is the Day which the Lord hath made, let us be glad and rejoice therein" (Ps. 117).

VI. When it was late and the disciples were gathered together Jesus came and stood in the midst and said to them: "Peace be to you."—John xx.

See the Eleven gathered together at night in the Upper Chamber discussing the events of the day. The women's story had not been believed, but now Peter has seen the Lord, and unbelief is giving way to trembling hope and joy. See Peter in the midst confirming his brethren according to our Lord's injunction. See the door opening, and the two disciples from Emmaus coming in. They find a very different state of things from what they left in the morning. Before they can speak, the rest cry out: "The Lord is risen indeed, and hath appeared to Simon." Watch them listening to Peter, and then, as the Eleven crowd round, adding their own testimony, telling "what things were done in the way, and how they knew Him in the breaking of bread."

Notice how the doors are shut for fear of the Jews. All noises without are hushed, for it is late. And still the disciples tell and hear unsatisfied the joyful news. Those who have seen our Lord repeat their tale again and again. Those who have not seen Him listen with beating hearts and wistful eyes. Oh that they, too, might look upon Him risen from the dead!

See! See! There in His wonted place—with radiant wounds in hands, and feet, and side—there with the smile they know so well—He stands. He looks with love upon them all. And hark! He speaks: "Peace be to you. It is I, fear not."

To us, too, He comes at Benediction, when it is late. Dear evening visit of our Lord, how did our forefathers get on without it? How we should miss it now! Is it like His coming to the little flock in Jerusalem gathered together within closed doors for fear of their enemies? Or like His visits to the sick and the sad when He was on earth? Or does it recall John's vision of "One like to the Son of Man in the midst of the golden candlesticks?" Or the eternal Benediction, where the Blessed with their harps and golden vials full of odours fall down before the Lamb and sing with a loud voice: "The Lamb that was slain is worthy to receive power, and divinity, and wisdom, and strength, and honour, and glory, and benediction. To Him that sitteth on the throne, and to the Lamb benediction, and honour, and glory, and power for ever and ever. Amen" (Apoc. 5.)

Perhaps it is like all these. There is the stealing away at nightfall from those who believe not in the Divine Presence amongst us: the gathering round the empty place where He is wont to stand: the hush…and then the sudden Coming, and the burst of joy and triumph. "The disciples were glad when they saw the Lord." And so are we.

He stands "in the midst." Of whom? Of His servants, little and great—the poor, the outcast, the heavy laden, the little children, as in the days of His life on earth. And now as then they bring to Him all manner of troubles, doubts, plans, difficulties, needs of every sort. Some come to Him for the souls confided to them; some for their own. Some to have their joy sanctified by His blessing: others to lay down their burden awhile at His feet. Some few there are who come to Him, not for His promised refreshment, but *for Himself*, to pour out their souls before Him in praise and thanksgiving, in sympathy, in reparation, in love.

"When it was late and the disciples were gathered together, Jesus came and stood in the midst, and said to them: "Peace be to you." Peace is His word to each and to all. Peace, His peace, in the midst of the world's rush and excitement and unrest: in the midst of its business, and its gaieties, its dangers and its cares.

Peace amid the storm of persecution, the heart-sinking at failure, the monotony of well-doing, and watching and waiting for better things.

Peace in the harder trials of life, the coldness of the nearest, the peril of the dearest.

Peace in the struggle with self—sharp, daily, unrelenting. In the struggle with God Himself; in the weary search for Him who hides; in the separation from Him who seems to have forsaken.

Peace is His word to us all. Peace, like the rays of His monstrance, radiates from Him on every side. How could it be otherwise when He Himself is in our midst. "It is I, fear not. It is I Myself. Peace I leave with you, My peace I give unto you; not as the world giveth do I give unto you. Let not your heart be troubled, nor let it be afraid (John 14). If the world hates you, know that it hath hated Me before you…The servant is not greater than his Master (John 15). In the world you shall have distress, but have confidence, I have overcome the world…You will indeed have sorrow, but I will see you again, and your heart shall rejoice, and your joy no man shall take from you" (John 16).

We shall see Him "*in Patria*" when time shall be no more…and the mystery of God shall be finished (Apoc. 10). And I heard a great voice from the throne saying: Behold the tabernacle of God with men, and He will dwell with them. And they shall be His people; and God Himself with them shall be their God" (Apoc. 21).

"Come up higher," will be the sweet invitation to the eternal Benediction, where is "the voice of harpers harping on their harps (Apoc. 14): where the Temple is filled with smoke from the Majesty of God (Apoc. 15): where the great multitude which no man can number, of all nations and tribes, and peoples and tongues, stand before the throne in sight of the Lamb, and cry with a loud voice: "Salvation to our God who sitteth upon the throne and to the Lamb…Amen. Benediction, and glory, and wisdom, and thanksgiving, honour, and power and strength to our God for ever and ever. Amen" (Apoc. 7).

Shall we think, then, amid that glory and that peace, of the days when we gathered round the little throne on earth, "the tabernacle of God with men," to behold "the Mystery of God," to wait for His coming in the midst of us, and to hear Him say: "Peace be to you"?

> VII. I am risen and am still with thee.—Ps. cxxxviii.

> Broken by our unkindness, Heart of Christ.
>   Truest of friends,
> Thou speedest back to us, as though 'twere Thine
>   To make amends.
> To comfort and to gladden, all Thy task,
>   Upbraiding not;
> All wrongs, all memories save those of love
>   Past and forgot.

VIII. See My hands and feet, that it is I Myself; handle and see.—Luke xxiv.

When all was over on Friday afternoon, and the body of their Victim lay lifeless and cold in the grave, the priests, fearful of His assurance that He would rise from the dead the third day, "made the sepulchre sure, sealing the stone, and setting guards."

But "He that dwelleth in Heaven shall laugh at them: and the Lord shall deride them" (Ps. 2).

Very early on the first day of the week, while it was yet dark, our Lord rose again. His sacred body, united once more to the Soul, rose glorious and immortal, every vestige of its humiliation gone. He rose in stillness and in solitude: only legions of adoring angels, and perhaps the holy souls from Limbo, to witness His Resurrection. His hour of triumph had come. The most glorious victory earth has ever seen was His, a victory that by proving His Divinity beyond the possibility of cavil, was to become the central point of the Church's faith, so that the preaching of the Gospel, was to be called the preaching of the Resurrection. Yet He would have no human eye as witness, no stir in the tomb, nothing to give notice by the faintest sign of what had passed within.

How differently we should have arranged His triumph! There were a million and a half or two millions of His people in Jerusalem. He might, had he so willed, have roused them from slumber by a terrific earthquake, which, if it did not shake the city into ruins, would have hurried them panic-stricken out of their dwellings into the surrounding valleys. Then, in the sight of King Herod, and the Governor, and priests, and Pharisees, of the vast multitude out of every nation under Heaven, He might have risen in glory from the tomb.

His thoughts are not our thoughts. The meekness and humility which had marked His earthly life seemed to cling to Him still. It was not Himself but His Angel who so terrified the guards that they became as dead men. He went quietly hither and thither among His friends, attractive and lovable as of old, but with a new tenderness, almost playfulness of manner now that the burden which had lain on His Heart for three and thirty years was lifted from Him. We see Him coming, and hiding, and calling them by their name, as when He went to the Sepulchre in search of Magdalen. Revealing Himself unexpectedly in the inn at Emmaus, or in the Upper Chamber on Mount Sion; or using His Omnipotence to provide breakfast for the disciples on the seashore of Tiberias. We find Him walking with them, eating with them, giving Himself to be handled by them, making it His study to convince them that He was in very deed the Master they had loved and followed in the days gone by. The natural questioning of their hearts would be: "Is it in truth the Lord Himself: If it is He, is He changed towards us by our miserable falling away from Him? Is the same familiar intercourse to be allowed us as before, the same confidence, the same love?" "Jesus knew that they had a mind to ask Him" these vital questions, and He anticipates them. "Peace be to you. It is I, fear not. See that it is I Myself. Handle Me and see, for a spirit hath not flesh and bones as you see Me to have. And when He had said this He showed them His hands and His feet" (Luke 24).

The Resurrection restores Him to them the same as before, if anything, more tender, because there was more to overlook, more need to reassure. What a delight it is to see Him come back to us *Himself*, unchanged, unchilled by the touch of death, unsevered from the sympathies of earth by the glorious state on which He has entered; no whit less human because now the Divinity displays itself—"Jesus yesterday, to-day, and the same for ever" (Heb. 13).

There are hearts so wrung with anguish by the leave-taking at the grave, that they refuse to believe in the survival of earth's dear ties beyond. They are not heartbroken because they deny themselves this consolation: but because they are heartbroken they will not accept it. To such as these our Lord offers His Sacred Human Heart after the Resurrection for their instruction and comfort. What loving eagerness He shows to be with His "brethren" once again. He abridges as far as possible the three days of separation. He anticipates the appointed meeting in Galilee by appearing six times at least on the very day of His Resurrection. He hastens from one to another of His friends. The thought uppermost in His mind seems to be the happiness His new and glorious life will bring to those He loves. His Resurrection is not the pledge only, it is the prototype of ours: "It hath not yet appeared what we shall be. But we know that we shall be like to Him" (I. John 3). Does not this suffice to satisfy and more than satisfy every desire? We shall be like Him. In retaining all that was noble and beautiful of the affections of earth; in the intensified because purified love of those bound to us by the ties of kindred and friendship; in sympathy with them closer and tenderer than any we know now—we shall be like Him.

"We may lift up our lightened hearts, then, to those who have gone before us "with the sign of faith and rest in the sleep of peace," remembering they are ours still and are to be restored to us one day as ours. "The God of all consolation" will give back to us those from whom we were parted for a time, dearer beyond measure for the parting, and for the new grace and beauty that have blossomed out in the sunshine of their eternal life. They will meet us at the gates of Heaven and we shall know them at once as our own. No need for them to say as they greet us with loving welcome: "See that it is I myself."

And God shall wipe away tears from all eyes: and death shall be no more, nor mourning, nor crying, nor sorrow shall be any more, for the former things are passed away.—Apoc. xxi.

IX. Ought not Christ to have suffered these things, and so to enter into His glory?—Luke xxiv.

See our Lord rising triumphant from the grave on Easter Day. See those sacred members radiant with the glory of their new life. Each has gone through its Passion and borne its share, suffering in its appointed place, for the appointed time, patiently, perseveringly, to the end. Each has been in full sympathy with the Head. Fittingly, then, does each share in the glory that now from that glorious Head flows down upon all.

Thus was it with the members of His mystical body who had stood round the Cross. The pain of each had been foreseen, measured out, appointed from eternity. And so was the joy that from their Head irradiated all, not gladdening all alike, but in proportion to the sufferings and dispositions of each. There was the joy of the holy women, the joy of Magdalen, the Mother's joy, like her love, immeasurably outstripping all.

Thus will it be with each and every one of His members unto the end. Therefore St. Peter bids us rejoice when we suffer with Christ "that when His glory shall be revealed we may also be glad with exceeding joy" (I. Peter 4). To be with Jesus of Nazareth costs for a little while. But it is to be our joy throughout eternity. To all who are faithful to Him here He says as to His dear apostles: "You now indeed have sorrow, but I will see you again and your heart shall rejoice, and your joy no man shall take from you" (John 16).

The Divine Child made His offering in the Temple with the knowledge that it would be accepted to the full. When the time came for Him to redeem the pledge He had given us, He was ready. "I do not resist: I have not gone back" (Isaias 50). And when His chalice had been drained to the dregs, and Easter morning had dawned, and He was striving on that Sabbath day's walk to instruct and cheer two of His disciples to whom the Passion had been a scandal, He said simply: "Ought not Christ to have suffered these things?" He was but fulfilling His engagement. Was it not to be expected of Christ that He would have a suffering life and a death of shame?

We can trust our Lord thoroughly. We can always depend on Him. What He undertakes He will carry through. What He promises He will fulfil. Can the same be said of me? Am I as good as my word? I have undertaken to follow Him, bearing my cross. When the cross comes to me in my daily life, can I say with Him: "I do not resist: I have not gone back. Ought not I to suffer these things"?

From first to last throughout the history of the elect the law holds good—death the road to resurrection and eternal life, and the only road. Are Enoch and Elias at least to be exempt? We might think so when we read of the stupendous powers given to them in the days of their prophecy: "I will give unto My two witnesses, and they shall prophesy a thousand two hundred sixty days…And if any man will hurt them, fire shall come out of their mouths, and shall devour their enemies. And if any man will hurt them, in this manner must he be slain. These have power to shut heaven and they have power over waters to turn them into blood, and to strike the earth with all plagues as often as they will" (Apoc. 11). How, then, shall these witness to the Lamb that was slain? How shall these servants be as their Master?

"And when they shall have finished their testimony, the beast that ascendeth out of the abyss, shall make war against them, and shall overcome them and kill them. And their bodies shall lie in the streets of the great city where their Lord also was crucified...for three days and a half. And they that dwell upon the earth shall rejoice over them and make merry...And after three days and a half, the spirit of life from God entered into them. And they stood upon their feet, and great fear fell upon them that saw them...And they went up to heaven in a cloud, and their enemies saw them" (*Id.*).

"As you are partakers of the sufferings of Christ, so shall you be also of the consolation" (II. Cor. 1). "If we suffer, we shall also reign with Him" (II. Tim. 2). Such is the universal law of Christ's kingdom. Have I any wish but to fulfil it, when, and how, and in the measure appointed for me?

X. Christ is risen from the dead, the first fruits of them that sleep.—i Cor. xv.

(1) God hath both raised up the Lord, and will raise up us also by His power (I. Cor. 6).

(2) Know you not that your bodies are the members of Christ? Glorify and bear God in your body (Id).

(3) We look for that life which God will give to those that never change their faith from Him (Tobias 2).

(4) We are now the sons of God; and it hath not yet appeared what we shall be. We know that when He shall appear we shall be like to Him, because we shall see Him as He is (I. John 3).

(5) If we believe that Jesus died and rose again, even so them who have slept through Jesus will God bring with Him (Thess. 4).

(6) Wherefore expect Me, saith the Lord in the day of My Resurrection that is to come…In that day thou shalt not be ashamed For all thy doings wherein thou hast transgressed against Me…The Lord will rejoice over thee with gladness, He will be silent in His love, He will be joyful over thee in praise (Sophon. 3).

(7) In that day you shall see the difference between the just and the wicked: between him that serveth God, and him that serveth Him not (Malach. 3).

(8) Fight the good fight of faith; lay hold on eternal life whereunto thou art called (I. Tim. 6).

(9) Keep yourselves in the love of God (Jude 1). And wait for His Son from Heaven, whom He raised from the dead, Jesus who hath delivered us from the wrath to come (I. Thess. 1).

(10) I know that my Redeemer liveth, and in the last day I shall rise out of the earth. And I shall be clothed again with my skin, and in my flesh I shall see my God. Whom I myself shall see, and my eyes shall behold, and not another: this my hope is laid up in my bosom (Job 19).

The Ascension

I. Sing ye to God, sing a psalm to His name: make a way for Him who ascendeth upon the west: the Lord is His name.—Ps. lxvii.

At length He appeared to the Eleven as they were at table: and He upbraided them with their incredulity and hardness of heart, because they did not believe them who had seen Him after He was risen again…

And He led them out as far as Bethania. And lifting up His hands He blessed them. And it came to pass whilst He blessed them He departed from them; and while they looked on He was raised up, and a cloud received Him out of their sight; and He was carried up to heaven, and sitteth on the right hand of God.

And while they were beholding Him going up to heaven, behold two men stood by them in white garments, who also said: Ye men of Galilee, why stand you looking up to heaven? This Jesus who is taken up from you into heaven shall so come as you have seen Him going into heaven.

And they, adoring, went back into Jerusalem with great joy, from the mount which is called Olivet. (Luke 24; Mark 16; Acts 1.)

See the disciples standing round our Lord on Olivet. With them His Mother and the faithful women. How absorbed are all in their contemplation of Him! How utterly forgotten is the earth and all it contains!

Feel the freshness of the breeze up on this height.

Taste the peace and happiness of the little group. The joy of belonging to our Lord; of being among His friends; of having made sacrifices for Him.

Admire the unselfish love that makes their faces so bright, their hearts so happy as they come down the Mount—alone.

> II. Be Thou exalted, O God, above the heavens,
> and Thy glory above all the earth.—Ps. lvi.

The forty days are over. What days they have been for the disciples! Any time they might expect a visit from their Master. In His absence they longed for Him. When He came, they feasted their eyes upon His glorious beauty, and hung upon His lips, and poured out their souls at His feet! Before His Passion He had said to them: "I have many things to say to you, but you cannot bear them now." During the forty days He has said these many things. He has been speaking to them of the Kingdom of God, that spiritual Kingdom of which they are to be under Him the founders, and which by their labours they are to extend to the ends of the earth. Now that the Resurrection has set the seal of the Divinity on His mission and His words, and solidly established their faith and trust in Him, they can bear to hear of the great things they are to suffer for His Name's sake. How sweet has been the intercourse between the Master and the disciples during these blessed days.

And now the last of them, Thursday, has come. The Eleven are at table when He appears to them. There is something very homely and tender in His choosing this time for coming into their midst. As if He would make up to them for the sadness of that Last Supper when He had to break to them that He was going away. To what lengths His condescension goes on this last morning on earth of His glorious and immortal life. We are expressly told that He ate with them. It is perhaps conceivable that He should thus humble Himself at His first appearance on Easter Day, when "they being troubled and affrighted supposed that they saw a spirit." But, after forty days, when "by many proofs" they have been convinced that He who came in and went out amongst them was in very deed their Lord and Master—what need of such loving familiarity now!

"And He upbraided them with their incredulity and hardness of heart because they did not believe them who had seen Him after He was risen again." How His Sacred Heart resented the want of faith! And they knew it. When, in that early morning, He provided their breakfast on the seashore, and "cometh and taketh bread, and giveth them, and fish in like manner, none of them who wore at meat durst ask Him: 'Who art Thou?' knowing that it was the Lord" (John 21).

"Durst"—for the only fault He could bring Himself to rebuke in those glad days was doubt, fear, slowness of heart to recognise Him as the same He had ever been to them. Was there not everything to reassure them? The well-known voice and salutation, the dear familiar words in which He was wont to calm their fears, the same Divine courtesy, the same gracious condescension, so natural, so sweet, that the condescension scarcely appeared, the human affectionateness and sympathy with their joys and pains that had marked all His dealings with them during the three years of intimate companionship—all this they found again, heightened by an indescribable charm after the Resurrection. It was the recognition of the old ways, and tones, and actions, as He chid, and taught, and comforted, and walked, and ate with them, that brought home at last to their slow hearts that it was in very truth Jesus Christ, yesterday, and to-day, and the same for ever.

Thus He showed Himself to them in the last visit. And eating with them He commanded them that they should not depart from Jerusalem, but should wait for the promise of the Father, "which you have heard," saith He, "by My mouth."

"And He led them out as far as Bethania," the part of Olivet that went by this name.

See them leaving the Supper Room together. When last they had gone thence with Him, it was to witness the beginning of His Passion under the olive trees. Now, along the same road, they go to be spectators of His triumph. Through the crowded streets they follow their Master, visible to themselves alone. Across Kedron, and past the Garden of Gethsemane. See Him, as He begins to ascend Olivet, looking down into the Garden where He lay in agony, sorrowful even unto death. He slackens His pace as the summit of the Mount is reached, as if loath to leave the earth and the little flock to whom He is all in all. See Him speaking tenderly, now to one, now to another—a last word to Magdalen, to John, to Peter, to His Mother. How they all press round Him, as if they feel they are about to lose Him.

Look reverently on Him as He stands now on the mountain brow. The fresh breeze stirs His raiment and His hair. He is gazing into the distance. His thoughts seem far away. Beneath Him lie the scenes of His life on earth. To the north is Nazareth, where, when all things were in quiet silence, and night was in the midst of her course, He came to Mary. There are tears of human feeling in His eyes as He thinks of His home, and of the little shop up the village street where He worked those many years by Joseph's side. To the south is Bethlehem where He came unto His own and His own received Him not. South-west Egypt, recalling memories of His infancy and boyhood. How long He stands there, still and silent, looking round. The hillsides, the corn fields, the desert places, the crowded streets, the quiet lanes, where He went about doing good, teaching, healing, comforting—His Heart yearns over them all.

At his feet is the Garden where He prayed that His chalice might pass from Him; where He accepted the Father's Will. Yonder are the pillar and the guard room where in His innocent flesh He satisfied for the sins of men. Trending westward, the road to Calvary, where He became the pattern of the suffering and the heavy laden, to the end of time. And there, outside the walls rose the hard deathbed where He taught us how to die.

Our Lord looks over the scenes of His life on earth and sees that everywhere He has perfectly fulfilled the Father's Will. "I have glorified Thee on the earth. I have finished the work Thou gavest Me to do. And now glorify Thou Me, O Father, with the glory which I had, before the world was, with Thee" (John 17).

His eyes turn again to His disciples. Lifting up His hands He blesses them, and rises into the air. He rises slowly. Up into the blue heavens He mounts, till a cloud receives Him out of their sight.

See them gazing after Him. Long, long after the cloud has sailed away, and all trace of Him has gone, they stand there motionless. "He was carried up to heaven, and sitteth on the right hand of God." And He has carried thither with Him all their interests, and affections, their very life. How can they bring down their gaze to earth again? Suddenly two men stand by them in white garments, who say: "Ye men of Galilee, why stand you looking up to heaven? This Jesus who is taken up from you into heaven, shall so come as you have seen Him going into Heaven."

"Why stand you looking up to heaven?" O Angels, what a question! Where should they look but into that heaven whither He has gone? What comfort is left for them here? Dark and lonely earth will be to them now. And yet they are not left without consolation. It is to be found in four things. In the glory of their Lord who has reached the end of His painful course and is now seated at the right hand of God. In the promise of His return. In the Comforter He will send them. In the work they are to do for Him. The disciples open their hearts to this comfort. "They adoring went back into Jerusalem with great joy," we are told.

Not the Mother only, from whom we expect the highest heroism of generosity, but those also who gathered round her as they went down the Mount together. Looking into her face, they caught her spirit of unselfishness, her joy in His glory, her zeal for the souls He came to save. They felt they must keep near her to sustain their souls on hers. With her they re-crossed Kedron, and threaded their way through the streets back to the Supper Room, there to await the coming of the Paraclete.

> III. God is ascended with jubilee, and the Lord with the sound of trumpet—Ps. xlvi.

> Rise, King of Glory, rise
> Unto Thy Throne!
> No power, no praise, no prize,
> But is Thine own.
> And we are Thine, Thy race,
> Thy brethren we;
> Lord, in Thy dwelling-place
> We, too, must be!

> IV. While they looked on He was carried up to heaven and sitteth on the right hand of God. —Acts i, Luke xxiv, Mark xvi.

Let us follow our Lord in thought from the moment when the cloud hides Him from the sight of the disciples. The day will come when we shall follow Him in body and soul even as we see Him going into heaven.

Look around. Myriads of Angels, those elder sons of God, are flocking earthward, eager to hail as King, Him who has repaired their ranks. And, pressing close in His train, nearer to Him even than His Angels, is a great multitude that no man could number—souls from Limbo and from Purgatory, the just made perfect, from Adam and Eve, and Abraham and David, to St. Joseph, and the good thief.

See the happy commingling for the first time of angelic and human spirits; how affectionately the Angels associate with those who are "a little lower" only than themselves by reason of their closer relationship with Him who is Head of all, the First- Born among many brethren.

Watch the grand procession as it sweeps onward to the eternal gates. Hear the sounds of praise and congratulation on every side. The chariot of God is attended by ten thousand, thousands of them that rejoice. The Lord is among them in the holy place. Ascending on high, Thou hast led captivity captive" (Ps. 67).

"Sing ye to God, ye kingdoms of the earth, sing ye to the Lord. Sing ye to God who mounteth above the heaven of heavens to the east. His magnificence and His power is in the clouds" (*Id.*).

Hear the summons to the warders of the heavenly City; "Lift up your gates, O ye princes, and be ye lifted up, O eternal gates; and the King of Glory shall enter in.

"Who is this King of Glory?

"The Lord who is strong and mighty; the Lord mighty in battle" (Ps. 24).

Kneel on the threshold of heaven as He enters with His train. Stoop down and kiss "the place of His feet." Beg Him to carry before the throne of God all your desires and affections. And to grant you now such grace, that when on the Last great Day all heaven shall pour out to the Judgment, and He shall return with the elect, you may be one of His suite.

O my Lord, remember me now that Thou art entering Thy Kingdom. Among its millions, remember me. Among its many mansions find a little place for me, that where Thou art I may be with Thee and see Thy glory. Give me grace to rule my life on Thine, that Thou mayst not be ashamed to acknowledge me for one of Thy members when Thou shalt come in the majesty of Thy Father and of the holy Angels.

<blockquote>V. "I ascend to My Father and to your Father."—John xx.</blockquote>

How dear to Thee, Lord, is Thy office as Head of our race! How Thou dost love to draw us into close companionship with Thee, to communicate to us all that is communicable in the privileges of sonship, to identify our interests with Thine!

My Father and your Father. He, the Elder Brother, bids us put on His likeness; clothe ourselves with His merits; offer the acceptable gifts He places in our hands, that we may win the blessing which is the birthright of the First-Born.

My Father and your Father. The adopted children are led up to our common Father by the Eternal Son for the embrace which is the right of every child.

My Father and your Father. We, the prodigal children are reconciled to the Father we have abandoned and outraged, by Him who does always the things that please Him.

<blockquote>VI. O clap your hands, all ye nations, shout unto God with the voice of joy.—Ps. xlvi.</blockquote>

Yes, all ye nations, for all are His redeemed, bought with a great price. Clap your hands, shout for joy; our Redeemer having risen from the dead dieth now no more; pain and sorrow shall no more come near Him.

It is all over, dear Lord, all over. No more torture for Thy sacred body; no more anguish for Thy generous Soul. Beneath the olive trees but forty days ago Thou didst accept

Thy cruel Passion: "The chalice which My Father hath given Me, shall I not drink it?" Now, on Olivet again, ascending in glory to the right hand of the Father, the cry of Thy Heart in Its overflowing gladness is: "My chalice which inebriateth, how goodly is it!" (Ps. 22).

Past for ever is that baptism with which Thou hadst to be baptized. Thou art no more straitened, for now it is accomplished. "The scourge shall not come nigh Thy dwelling" (Ps. 90). Thine enemies shall rage and devise vain things…and Thou Lord, dwelling in heaven, shalt laugh at them (Ps. 2). Past is all the humiliation and the woe Thy Incarnation involved. But not past, never to be past, are its blessed fruits. Never to be past Thy triumph as Conqueror over sin and hell. Never to be past the song of praise that goes up to Thee from Thine elect. Never past Thy work of intercession for us at the right hand of the Father—the pleading of Thy Wounds, the light, and strength, and consolation that flow from them to the uttermost parts of the earth.

And never to be past, nay rather to begin from this hour, my personal return to Thee for the redemption Thou hast brought—a redemption as much for me as if it had been wrought for me alone. Nay, is it not more to me a thousand times, than if it had profited no other? Is it not more to me that all whom I love, that this dear human family, every member of it, was under those outstretched arms on Calvary and drawn into their embrace?

O clap your hands, all ye nations, shout unto God with the voice of joy. And you, holy and happy ones, who have secured for ever the fruits of that Redemption, who have washed your robes and made them white in the Blood of the Lamb, praise Him for us till we join you and unite our voices with yours. Even here in this vale of tears your song of praise reaches us, that we may echo it however faintly: "Thou art worthy, O Lord our God, to receive glory, and honour, and power" (Apoc. 4)…because Thou wast slain, and hast redeemed us to God in Thy Blood, out of every tribe, and tongue, and people, and nation. The Lamb that was slain is worthy to receive power, and divinity, and wisdom, and strength, and honour and glory, and benediction (Apoc. 5). We give Thee thanks, O Lord God Almighty, who art, and who wast, and who art to come; because Thou hast taken to Thee Thy great power, and Thou hast reigned (Apoc. 11).

> VII. While they looked on He was carried up, and a cloud received Him out of their sight.—Acts i.

Can we imagine a way of withdrawing His presence from this world better fitted to draw their hearts after Him? He might have sent an Angel to say He had ascended, as one was sent to say He was risen. He might have met them in the Supper Room and there made them His farewell. But to gather them round Him and lead them up to a peak of earth, and thence to rise slowly above their heads, letting their eyes follow Him till the cloud received Him out of their sight— was not this to attract their hearts vehemently whither He had gone! Was it not to link together Heaven and earth, in a union that shall never again be broken! Earth stood on tiptoe to lift Him up: Heaven stooped to receive Him.

What a life of paradoxes is the life of the Word made Flesh! God become man; the Creator to have a created nature; the Almighty to be helpless and weak; the All Wise to learn; the All Perfect to increase in grace before God and man; Life to die; the most faithful of friends to leave us, and leaving, to remain with us all days!

And here on Olivet, drawing His disciples after Him in heart and desire; yet sending them back into Jerusalem, to long absence from Him, to struggle and persecution, labours and death "with great joy."

In the Eucharist and the Paraclete we might find an explanation of the joy. But by another paradox. These gentle forces were to sustain, not to satisfy. They were to maintain for ever in their hearts and in the hearts of His disciples to the end of time, the longing desire to see face to face Him who, beneath His veils, is the source of all their desires; the pining for that "abiding City" which "the Spirit Himself asketh for us with unspeakable groanings" (Rom. 8).

VIII. If you be risen with Christ, seek the things that are above where Christ sitteth at the right hand of God. Mind the things that are above, not the things that are upon the earth.—Coloss. iii.

See the disciples wending their way towards the Mount of Olives: He in their midst, visible to them, not to His enemies. Note how He is literally the one thought, the one love of them all. How every aim, desire, affection, centres in Him. How He is the bond of union among so many of different ranks, callings, characters. See the radiant peace on every face. Look into each heart and see how joy and confidence reign supreme; how the world with its pleasures and honours is not so much despised as utterly ignored by these men of lowly station.

Why? Because being risen with Christ, they seek the things that are above, whither their Lord is ascending to sit at the right hand of God. The love of Christ has drawn them out and freed them from the absorbing love of self. His views, His Will, His service, have taken the place of personal considerations. How proud they are of Him. And of being His. How they look to Him, lean upon Him, trust to Him the future so lowering, so unprovided for. What matter if life is to be full of peril and pain, if goods, home, friends, strength, life itself, have to be sacrificed for Him! He will be with them through it all. He will make up to them for all. He will be ready to receive them when their work for Him is done. In a little while they will be with Him in His Kingdom. Oh that that hour were come now!

But six weeks ago all His acquaintance and the women that had followed Him from Galilee, stood afar off beholding what seemed to be the end of all their hopes. It was the eve of the Pasch. The rejoicings of the morrow were mockery and misery to them. On the first day of the week they rose from troubled sleep to face life again, their hearts weighted with a sorrow beyond the power of heaven or earth to lighten. So it seemed. But the next day when they rose—if indeed there was rest for any of them that night that followed the Resurrection—and the next day, and the next, and as day succeeded day—what a change! If earth looked dark now, it was because the light of His face had dulled all else to them. No loss could sadden them: no persecution shake them; nothing could fetter the freedom or quench the joy of hearts to which their risen Lord was all in all.

Calvary had crushed them to the earth: it had not raised them to heaven. Unless mind and heart open to the grace that comes with a great sorrow, this will not work detachment—a hopeless, bitter disgust of life, perhaps, but this is not detachment. Detachment is a bright grace, that frees the soul from earthly ties, not to leave it unsupported and unsatisfied, but to bear it swiftly to God. It does not kill or blunt the affections, but purifies and intensifies them that they may cleave with all their strength to the Sovereign Good, the All-sufficing God. Thus the work, begun by sorrow, must be perfected by hope and love. The Easter sun must follow upon the three hours of darkness, as it did for our Lord's first disciples. Having Him, they needed nothing beside. Even those who had not yet seen Him were happy in the thought of His happiness and in the promise that they should see Him soon.

And when the cloud on Olivet had taken Him from their sight, they were joyful still. We are told expressly that they went back into Jerusalem "with great joy." "And they were always in the Temple praising and blessing God." The sensible loss His Ascension had brought to them was forgotten in their exultation at His triumph. And He was with them yet, beneath the veils. Day and night they could go to Him for light, for strength, for every needful grace. The trials of earth fell lightly on hearts that were in Heaven with their Treasure. Their conversation, their interests were there. They were risen with Christ and sought "the things that are above where Christ is sitting at the right hand of God."

We, too, are His disciples—why should it not be thus with us?

> IX. This Jesus who is taken up from you into heaven, shall so come as you have seen Him going into heaven.—Acts i.

What would her Child be like? was Mary's constant thought during the time of her Expectation before His birth. How would He look into her face? How would she dare to look on Him, nurse Him, swathe Him, fold Him in her arms? Would she be dazzled and overpowered by the glory streaming from Him? Thus the Greek liturgy makes her muse and question. And the answer is: "Wait, Blessed Mother, wait."

With greater reason would she ponder thus in her heart during the forty hours of her second Expectation, when she was awaiting her Son's return to her from the grave, His Birthday to a new and immortal life. She knew that the Divinity, hitherto concealed, was now to manifest Itself. How could she dare to look upon Him in His glory?

We, too, are expecting the Coming of Christ.

We expect Him daily in His inspirations and secret visits to our souls.

We expect His descent on to the altar in the one, unending Sacrifice.

We expect Him in Holy Communion, veiled in the Host, as shrouded in human flesh at Bethlehem.

We expect Him at the General Judgment on the Last Day, when He will come in His majesty amid the clouds of heaven, and every eye shall see Him.

We expect Him at the Particular Judgment in the very moment of death. Life from first to last is our expectation of this dread coming to us as Judge. How often does it find us echoing our Mother's questioning: "When will He come to me? And how?"

When He has not told me. I have to be always watching, always listening for the sound of His feet. "Watch," He says to me, "for you know not when the Lord of the house cometh, at even, or at midnight, or at cock-crowing or in the morning;

lest coming on a sudden He find you sleeping. And what I say to you I say to all: Watch" (Mark 13).

How He will come depends on myself. Lord, give me grace to live so faithful a child of holy Church, that her prayer for me may he heard in the hour when my trembling soul shall go forth from the body into the house of its eternity:

"As thy soul goeth forth from the body, may the bright company of Angels meet thee; may the judicial senate of Apostles greet thee; may the triumphant army of white-robed Martyrs come out to welcome thee; may the band of glowing Confessors, crowned with lilies, encircle thee; may the choir of Virgins, singing jubilees, receive thee…mild and festive may the aspect of Jesus Christ appear to thee."

Meantime, we, too, like the Blessed Mother, are waiting. A servant of God summed up her life in the words: "I believe; I hope; I wait." We wait for Him, and work while we wait; all our work directed to Him, done for Him, ready to be left the moment He calls.

Our Lord, too, is waiting and expecting. He is standing at the open door of Heaven watching and listening for our coming. The songs of praise and jubilee within do not absorb Him. He looks down to earth; follows us hither and thither; sympathises with us in every trial and care. Wishes sometimes we had a little more desire to be with Him in the Home He is preparing for us. That our hearts would catch fire by contact with His. That we could be, not resigned only to die, but filled with desire to be dissolved and to be with Christ. That we would put more heart into the prayer He Himself has placed on our lips: "Thy Kingdom come." That our constant cry could be that of the Beloved Disciple: "Come, Lord Jesus!"

X. Who hath brought many children unto glory.—Heb. ii.

(1) In My Father's House there are many mansions (John 14). I go to prepare a place for you (Id). If I go to prepare a place for you, I will come again and will take you to Myself that where I am you also may be (*Id.*).

(2) Whither I go you know and the way you know (*Id.*).

(3) If you be risen with Christ seek the things that are above (Coloss. 3).

(4) Mind the things that are above where Christ is sitting at the right hand of God (*Id.*). When Christ shall appear who is your life, then you also shall appear with Him in glory (*Id.*).

(5) Yet a little while and a very little while and He that is to come, will come, and will not delay (Heb. 10).

(6) Behold, He cometh with the clouds, and every eye shall see Him (Apoc. I.).

(7) Behold, I come quickly, and My reward is with Me to render to every man according to his works (Apoc. 22).

(8) Behold, I come quickly, hold fast that which thou hast, that no man take thy crown (Apoc. 3).

(9) Be thou faithful unto death, and I will give thee the crown of life (Apoc. 2).

(10) Surely I come quickly (Apoc. 22). Amen. Come, Lord Jesus (*Id.*).

The Descent of the Holy Ghost

I. Thou gavest them Thy good Spirit to teach them.—2 Esdras ix.

And they, adoring, went back into Jerusalem with great joy. And when they were come in, they went up into an upper room, where abode Peter and John, James and Andrew, Philip and Thomas, Bartholomew and Matthew, James of Alpheus and Simon Zelotes, and Jude the brother of James. All these were persevering with one mind in prayer with the women, and Mary the Mother of Jesus, and with His brethren.

And they were always in the Temple, praising and blessing God.

And when the days of Pentecost were accomplished, they were all together in one place. And suddenly there came a sound from heaven, as of a mighty wind coming, and it filled the whole house where they were sitting. And there appeared to them parted tongues as it were of fire, and it sat upon every one of them; and they were all filled with the Holy Ghost. And they began to speak with divers tongues, according as the Holy Ghost gave them to speak (Luke 24; Acts 1).

Hear the sound of the mighty wind as it fills the Cenacle where the disciples are assembled.

See the tongues of fire on the heads of all; the peace of each radiant face. The Comforter has come!

Feel the joy of each heart as it communes in silence with Him who has more than satisfied its every need.

> II. If you being evil know how to give good gifts to your children, how much more will your Father from heaven give the good Spirit to them that ask Him!—Luke xi.

How hopeless, seemingly, was the prospect before the Eleven as they came slowly down from Olivet after witnessing the Ascension of their Divine Master! What Presence could compensate for His absence, or what power fit them for the work in front of them? But the Resurrection had done its work. It had taught them implicit reliance on their Master's word. He had promised them a Comforter able to take His place and to prepare them for the work they had to do. This was enough. They went up into the Cenacle and began their preparation for Him who was to be sent.

See them in that Upper Chamber hallowed by so many mysteries; where they had heard the first Mass said by Christ

Himself, and been ordained priests to do in commemoration of Him what He had done; where they had received the power to forgive sins, and the commission to teach all nations. Gathered round Mary, the Mother of Jesus, as the Scripture is careful to tell us, and Peter, now Vicar of Christ, they begin the first novena, and enter on the first Christian retreat. The details St. Luke gives us enable us to see them in their solitude and follow them in their work of preparation.

They "were all together in one place…an upper room," far from the distractions of the world. They "were always" (*i.e.*, very frequently) "in the Temple, praising and blessing God." "Persevering with one mind in prayer," under the headship of Peter, and "with Mary the Mother of Jesus." By union of mind and heart, prayer in common, submission to authority, the motherly protection of Mary—thus did the first disciples prepare for the coming of the Holy Ghost. We must imitate them if we want Him to visit us.

We notice that the chief part of their preparation is prayer. And this, although the Holy Spirit has been promised. The promises of God are conditional. They suppose that we do our part.

See them together in their retreat. Now in silent prayer. Now listening to Peter's words. Now one by one at Mary's side getting a word of instruction or of counsel. And now, as the various hours of prayer come round, betaking themselves to the Temple for its services.

Watch our Lady on her return from Olivet retiring to a quiet corner of the Upper Room to be alone with God. What marvellous meditations hers will be. Her heart is filled with overwhelming joy in the Ascension. For she knows whence her Son is ascending, and whither. "If you loved Me you would indeed be glad, because I go to the Father," He said to His disciples. In proportion to her love was her gladness. She knew that of all the sons of men none had ever been or would ever be more truly an exile on earth than her Divine Child. None could feel that exile so keenly. With all His condescension to us, His willing companionship with us, His adoption of our ways, His interest in our labours and trials, He was alone. No one could rightly appreciate Him. No one could approach Him in sanctity, in hatred of sin, in weariness of soul at the wickedness and waywardness of men. No other could look out over the world from His level; measure with His standards; fathom the depths of His love; understand the aching of His Heart; respond with anything like adequateness to His affection and His desires. She herself, with all her nearness to Him and sympathy with Him, which as His Virgin Mother was her unshared privilege, remained at an infinite distance from Him. The Father alone could understand the Sacred Human Heart of His Son. Oh how glad she was because she loved Him so purely that He should go to the Father!

For her own sake, too, and for ours, she rejoiced. Because in ascending to heaven, her Son has gone before to show the way. Because He has taken the first fruits of His Redemption with Him into His Kingdom. Because we have now a Mediator ever living to make intercession for us before the throne of God.

She rejoiced, because the Ascension shows the value of pain and sacrifice endured for God's glory. With what joy she now recalls the hardships suffered with her Divine Son in Bethlehem, Egypt, Nazareth; the disgrace that came upon her as His Mother during the Passion,—along the way to

Calvary, at the foot of the Cross. She sees that to have been the companion of Christ in suffering is a higher dignity, a happier lot than any glory earth can give, that Heaven itself has nothing higher in which to glory. "Thou also wast with Jesus of Nazareth," is the mutual congratulation which the Blessed never tire of repeating to one another. It is a memory whose joy is ever fresh.

She prepared herself, then, for fresh labours and troubles. A new path opened out before her as she came down from Olivet, a path marked all along by sacrifice, like her road hitherto. How dull life must have looked to her when He was gone! Yet Mary's brave heart lived on and was content to live, even though absent from her Son, even though her heart was with her Treasure, so it was God's Will and for His greater glory. If a saint was ready to forego the immediate possession of God in heaven for the privilege of still doing Him some service on earth, how much more generously would Mary's heart accept the work allotted her of cherishing the orphan disciples, and helping them to spread far and wide the fruit of Christ's Redemption.

III. "These were all persevering in prayer."—Acts i.

And it came to pass that as He was in a certain place praying, when He ceased, one of His disciples said to Him: "Lord, teach us to pray, as John also taught his disciples" (Luke 11). It was the sight of His prayer that woke within the hearts of the Twelve the desire to pray, and to be taught how to pray. Long before, in the solitude of the holy Home at Nazareth, His first disciple had learned of Him this science to be desired above all others. What must prayer have been by His side, inspired by Him, aided by Him, with Him as her model and as the object of her prayer, with Him to hear and to grant! By Him, with Him, in Him, were all her petitions put up to the throne of God.

What reverence she learned of Him, what filial confidence, what fervour! See her face as she says the Our Father. Watch her at prayer in the Temple and in the Cenacle during this novena of preparation for the coming of the Holy Ghost. How does she pray? With exterior modesty, kneeling, her hands joined; with application of mind, with faith, with the certainty of obtaining. The humble persistence of the Canaanite woman won from our Lord the praise: "O woman, great is thy faith!" What was Mary's faith, what the fulness of hope, the humility, the perseverance with which she prayed! What, therefore, will have been the fruit of her prayer!

The Apostles and disciples strengthened their supplications by union with hers. They prayed with an intimate sense of their need; with an ardent desire of receiving the promised Comforter; with confidence that their prayer would be heard in God's good time. They prayed for gifts worthy of God; for all that was requisite to carry out His designs. If for temporal things, with freedom of heart, laying their needs trustfully before their Father in Heaven, casting their care on Him, relying on His Providence, knowing that He who is infinitely wise and good would give them all that was fitting, conforming themselves in all things spiritual and temporal to His good pleasure.

What is my daily prayer like? Does it in any respect resemble that of Mary and the disciples?

Holy Mary, Mother of God, pray for us sinners. Pray for me that my prayer may become more like thine. Get me light to see the needs of my soul that I may know what to pray for.

Remind me in time of temptation to turn at once to prayer. Teach me to convert anxieties, plans, everything into prayer. Help me to pray always with the reverence which is the fruit of faith. And with the trust of a child; commending to my Father who is in heaven all that concerns me and those who are dear to me; leaving to Him the time and the manner of His answer. Get me a trust that long delays do not dishearten, nor disappointments disturb. Get me perseverance in prayer to the end.

IV. "Persevering with one mind."—Acts i.

Now at last the disciples realised that their strength must be in union. Now they understood their Master's prayer for them: "that they may be one" (John 17). The Scripture emphasises this. "All were together...with the women, and with the Mother of Jesus and with His brethren. Peter rising up in the midst of *the brethren,* said (now the number of persons together was about one hundred and twenty): Men, brethren," etc. Henceforth we hear of no bickering among the Twelve. Peter as Head directs, even in so momentous a matter as the election of an apostle. The rest acquiesce with unquestioning loyalty. "Loving one another with the charity of brotherhood, with honour preventing one another" (Rom. 12). Each has his special claim to consideration—Andrew, the first chosen, "James, and Cephas, and John, who seemed to be pillars" (Galat. 2), John, the Beloved, "James, the brother of the Lord" (Galat. 1).

Mary, the object of profoundest veneration to all, is an example of submission to the Apostles. With what reverence and affability she treats them. What service she renders them. How she encourages them; solves their doubts with patience and charity; consoles them as a mother; helps them with fervent prayer. See how they bring to her both joys and sorrows, in every necessity having recourse to her, and never without consolation.

Do I, like our Lady, seek occasions of serving and helping others? Am I ready to bear defects? Do I brighten life to those around me; or the contrary? No one left Mary without having gained: could this be said of me? Is my conversation prudent, charitable, careful of the good name of the absent? Do I pray for others, for those especially who are confided to me and for whom I shall have to give an account?

V. With Mary the Mother of Jesus.—Acts i.

One petition summed up all Mary's desires during her preparation for Pentecost: "Thy Kingdom come!" It was the cry of her Son's Heart from the moment of the Incarnation. It is Its cry still from every Tabernacle, in every Mass, in the breast of every communicant. And will be till we "shall see the Kingdom of God coming in power" (Mark 8).

She prayed for herself, for the disciples, for the whole human family confided to her. For herself. We might have thought that further accessions of grace would be scarcely possible to Mary, who at fourteen, and before the overshadowing of the Holy Ghost at Nazareth, was full of grace. But the last word of the Spirit of God to us in Holy Scripture shows us our mistake: "He that is holy let him be sanctified still" (Apoc. 22). The capacity of the soul is indefinite. There is no point where we can say: Thus far and no farther.

We who find it hard, perhaps, to pray with anything like ardour for purely spiritual gifts, who fail to realise our plainest and most crying needs, can form no picture of the boundless horizons that open out before the soul that grace has lifted far above the things of earth. We have no conception of the grandeurs and beauties which it is given to her to contemplate and to desire. We do not even suspect the existence of the riches for which she is bidden to ask. Thus we cannot bring home to ourselves what "Thy Kingdom come" could mean on the lips of that fair creature of God whom He had possessed so fully from the beginning. Yet we can understand that if she is to be the channel of grace to the Church, the neck uniting the Head to the members, she must be, not only full of grace, but overflowing. As a fountain whence all may draw, she must be running over. As a queen, her riches must superabound that she may dispense on every hand. Therefore this holy one, like the last and lowest in the Kingdom of God, prayed: "Thy Kingdom come."

It is easier to realise what this prayer would mean when prayed for the Twelve. The evangelisation of the world was before them, and with wistful eyes they were looking towards the mountains whence their help should come. Can we imagine instruments less apt than those which God had provided for His hand? So little conscious of the character of their mission, that their last question before the Ascension was: "Lord, wilt Thou at this time restore the kingdom to Israel?" So narrow, that at the Last Supper they were disputing for precedence. So illiterate and uncouth, that their very name of Galilean was a reproach.

But the foolish things of the world had God chosen that He might confound the wise; and the weak things of the world that he might confound the strong; and things that are not that He might bring to nought things that are. That no flesh should glory in His sight (I. Cor. 1). The whole glory was to redound to that Holy Spirit who was now about to descend upon His chosen to fit them for His designs. It was for this descent that Mary's prayer went up with such a vehemence of supplication: "Thy Kingdom come!"

And she might add with her Divine Son: "Not for them only do I pray, but for them also who through their word shall believe" (John 17). In the purpose of God, she through whom the Redeemer came is the channel of grace to all the redeemed. With what ardour, then, will she desire for each the coming of that "Kingdom of God which is justice, and peace, and joy in the Holy Ghost" (Rom. 14). We have all of us had our share in our Mother's prayer for the coming of the Holy Spirit. Let us remind her of this and ask her to pray for the effect of that prayer now.

Holy Mary, Mother of God, pray for us sinners, now, that He may come to us and abide with us. We are not ready for His coming, but it belongs to a mother's homely office to prepare the children for a visit. Help us, thy needy children, as a good mother supplies her little ones from her own stores. Thou seest, Blessed Mother, how cold and careless we are, how wayward, slothful, selfish. He can and will change us if we dispose ourselves to receive Him. We put ourselves into thy hands. Make us ready for Him. Pray Him who overshadowed thee to descend upon us. Say to Him for each one of us: "Thy Kingdom come!"

VI. They were all filled with the Holy Ghost.—Acts ii.

See the assembly of one hundred and twenty on the morning of the fiftieth day, the Day of Pentecost. All are in silent prayer, waiting God's time, not knowing His hour is at hand. Notice, in the lowly place she has chosen, that handmaid of the Lord whom the Holy Ghost is about to overshadow for the second time.

Hark! a sound from heaven as of a mighty wind coming. Hear it filling the whole house where they are sitting. See the parted tongues, as it were of fire, upon the head of every one of them. See the sudden kindling of every countenance, testifying to the change that has been wrought within. All are filled with the Holy Ghost, according to the capacity and needs of each. He has recalled to their minds all that Christ our Lord had taught them. He has bestowed the gift of communicating to others what they have learned, and of being understood by men of every nation, tribe, and tongue. They have power to heal the sick, to raise the dead, to teach with authority and with force, to convince the intellect and to gain the will of those who hear them.

These gifts are necessary to them as preachers of the Gospel. But there are others more personal and precious. A marvellous change has been worked in themselves. In an instant the Holy Spirit has cleared away the obstacles He found in the soul of each. Like a mighty wind He has swept over them, vivifying, purifying, bracing. Like a consuming fire He has refined in an instant what was "of the earth earthly." Deeply-rooted prejudices of race, selfishness, intemperate zeal, jealousy, presumption—failings that come out again and again in the Gospel story, are gone, replaced by the charity of God that is poured forth in their hearts by the Holy Ghost who is given to them. Now they will boldly face the Jewish priests saying: "If it be just in the sight of God to hear you rather than God, judge ye" (Acts 4). Now they will go "from the presence of the Council rejoicing that they are accounted worthy to suffer reproach for the name of Jesus…and every day will cease not in the Temple and from house to house to teach and preach Christ Jesus."

Think of the humble gratitude, of the joyful praise that goes up to God from the hearts of all as they find in themselves the fruit of their Master's promise: "I will ask the Father and He will give you another Paraclete, that He may abide with you for ever…You shall know Him because He shall abide with you and shall be in you" (John 14).

If such were the gifts bestowed by the Holy Ghost on the Apostles, with what a plenitude of grace did He pour Himself forth on Mary in whom He found nothing to repel but all to invite Him. How He delighted in this perfect work; this supreme success from first to last: this beautiful one without spot or wrinkle, who alone among the works of His hands had loved her Creator with her whole heart and soul, with all her mind and with all her strength; this soul among whose "glorious riches" one gem still shone resplendent above all others—the humility that had enabled Him who is mighty to do great things for her!

Holy Mary, Spouse of the Holy Ghost, by the exceeding love with which He came to thee at Pentecost, pray for us, sinners, that to us, too, He may come, to purify, enlighten, heal, and enrich our needy souls.

VII. Grieve not the Holy Spirit of God.—Ephes. iv.

> Grieve not the Holy Spirit. If to-day
> Upon a treacherous path thy feet He stay,
>   Halt, and obey.
>
> If unto nobler tasks, a higher plane
> He beckon thee, spring forward to attain
>   The proffered gain.

> Deem it not light that God Himself should lead
> Thy laggard steps, and if to better speed
>   He urge, give heed.
>
> Commit to Him thy way. Upon Him cast
> Thy daily care. With Him, thine exile past,
>   Rejoice at last.

VIII. My Spirit shall be in the midst of you, fear not.—Aggeus ii.

(1) O children of Sion, rejoice and be joyful in the Lord your God; because He hath given you a teacher of justice (Joel 2).

(2) Desire of Him to direct thy ways, and that all thy counsel may abide in Him (Tobias 4).

(3) To-day if you shall hear His voice harden not your hearts (Ps. 94).

(4) Grieve not the Holy Spirit of God (Ephes. 4).

(5) Who hath resisted Him and hath had peace? (Job 9).

(6) The Spirit of the Lord shall come upon thee and thou shalt be changed into another man (I. Kings, 10).

(7) Cast me not away from Thy face, and take not Thy holy Spirit from me (Ps. 50).

(8) Give to Thy servant an understanding heart (III. Kings 3).

(9) Give me wisdom that sitteth by Thy throne (Wisd. 9).

(10) Send her out of Thy holy heaven, and from the throne of Thy Majesty, that she may be with me, and may labour with me, that I may know what is acceptable with Thee (*Id.*).

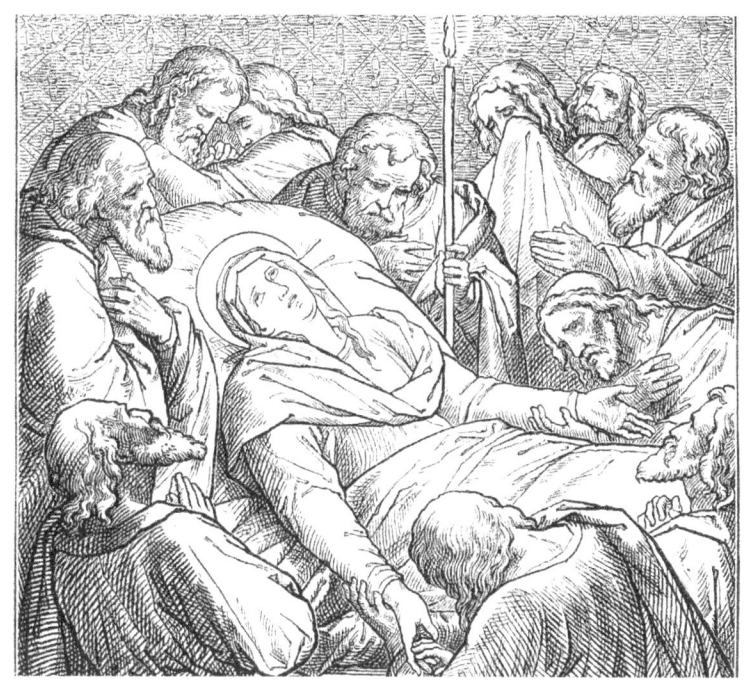

The Assumption of The Blessed Virgin

I "Arise, make haste, my love, my dove, my beautiful one, and come! The winter is now past, the rain is over and gone, the flowers have appeared in our land…Arise, my love, my beautiful one, and come!"—Cant. ii.

"Who is she that goeth up by the desert, as a pillar of smoke of aromatical spices, of myrrh, and frankincense? (Cant. 3)…flowing with delights, leaning upon her beloved? (Cant. 8).

"Who is she that cometh forth as the morning rising, fair as the moon, bright as the sun, terrible as an army set in array?" (Cant. 6).

See the soul of Mary winging its way to God.

See how it leaves the earth, not stainless only, but with its magnificent gifts developed to the utmost to the glory of Him who gave them.

Taste the sweetness of memory as Mary looks down on the scenes where her life was laid.

Feel the trembling eagerness with which she approaches the Throne of the Most High.

See her prostrate there, the handmaid of the Lord.

> II. Put off the garments of thy mourning and affliction,
> and put on the beauty and honour of that everlasting glory
> which thou hast from God.—Baruch v.

The last picture of our Lady in holy Scripture shows her seated among the disciples, awaiting the coming of the Holy Ghost. We find no further record of her in its pages, and only from the scanty notices of tradition can we learn anything of the eight, nine, twelve, fifteen, eighteen, or, as some say, twenty-four remaining years of her life on earth. Where she lived in Jerusalem has not come down to us. Some think her home was the Cenacle, which was hallowed by the institution of the Blessed Eucharist, the appearances of Christ after the Resurrection, and the Descent of the Holy Ghost. In the year A.D. 44, the persecution by Herod Agrippa broke out and, according to a very ancient tradition of the Church of Ephesus, St. John took our Lady thither for greater safety. It is a disputed point whether her death took place at Ephesus or at Jerusalem. Perhaps the balance of traditional evidence points to Jerusalem.

We might have thought the life of Mary on earth would close with that of her Divine Son at the Ascension. But there was a long term of exile to come. James, Stephen, many and many a faithful servant was called to his reward, while the Mother was kept waiting. Her heart was drawn two ways. Above, in the peace and glory of His Kingdom, was her Divine Son. On earth, amid temptations and dangers, were the children committed to her by Him. With greater reason than St. Paul she could say: "I am straitened between two, having a desire to be dissolved and to be with Christ…But to abide still in the flesh is needful for you. And having this confidence, I know that I shall abide and continue with you for your furtherance and joy of faith" (Philip 1).

She had a special office to discharge towards the infant Church. During the forty hours of desolation, from Friday afternoon to Easter morning, when their hopes were destroyed and their leaders scattered, the disciples fled to her motherly bosom for refuge and consolation. And when at the Ascension our Lord's sensible presence was finally withdrawn, she became the centre round which they instinctively gathered. She was a possession common to them all, a joy and protection, the benefit of which must have been simply incalculable. What a resource the Apostles found in her vigilance, her counsel, her knowledge of the designs of God; and in the motherly affection with which she placed all her spiritual treasures at their disposal. With what confidence they relied on the power of her prayer. They brought to her the converts who were daily added to the Church, and who found themselves surrounded by dangers of every kind. How eager these new disciples would be to see the Mother of their Saviour, to hear, as she alone could tell it, the story of Bethlehem and Egypt, and of the holy years at Nazareth. She was herself a living memory of the Three and Thirty Years, the closest of links with their

Redeemer. Those who had known Him would tell the less favoured how she recalled to them His ways, His speech, His manner of dealing with others, His very look.

What a continual grace her presence amongst them must have been. What they must have owed to the sanctity and example of the Mother of God. They saw her in adoration before the Blessed Sacrament, assisting at the unbloody Sacrifice, absorbed in her thanksgiving after Communion, visiting in company with the holy women the places sanctified by the footsteps of her Son. Whilst she remained to them who had been His inseparable companion for thirty years, who knew Him, understood Him, loved Him as no other could do, their Lord's presence seemed to linger on among them still.

She may seldom have been seen in public. Her life was mainly given to prayer and meditation on the mysteries in which she had so marvellous a part. But she will have been always ready with her motherly sympathy and help wherever danger threatened, whenever there was guidance or comfort to be given. Every new convert was sure of a welcome, of a willing ear to which he might confide the history of God's dealings with his soul, of a tender interest in all that touched him, of counsel exquisitely adapted to his need. She took them all to her motherly heart. She sustained the courage of the martyrs and of the faithful under persecution. She was the Refuge of sinners, the Comforter of the afflicted, the Mother of Good Counsel in difficult cases, the Perpetual Succour of all. Think what it must have been in doubts, and temptation, and persecution to be able in have recourse to the wisdom and the charity of the Mother of God!

And now the tidings were spreading through the Church that this sacred life could not be much further prolonged. The perfect acquiescence that made her accept the office assigned her towards the infant Church, could not check the pining of her soul after Him whom she loved:

"As the hart panteth after the waterbrooks, so panteth my soul alter Thee, O God. My soul hath thirsted after the strong, living God. When shall I come and appear before the face of God? (Ps 41).

"Who will give me the wings of a dove, and I will fly away and be at rest?" (Ps. 54).

"For Thee my soul hath thirsted, for Thee my flesh, O how many ways" (Ps. 62).

"Bring my soul out of prison that I may praise Thy Name" (Ps. 141).

In the first instant of her being, Mary loved God with a perfect love. This love had gone on increasing every moment of her life. It grew with every look at Jesus, every service rendered Him, every look, and word, and act of His during the long years they spent together. To what a height must that love have reached when she stood by His side on Olivet. When she saw Him ascending above her—without her, into His Kingdom. Only the hand of God that had sustained her on Calvary, and in the first transports of the Resurrection enabled her to love as she loved—and live on.

But the day came at last when the Church no longer needed her visible presence, when the measure of her merits was complete, when the Will of God that had imposed sacrifice for so many years, called her to rest and reward: "Arise, make haste, My love, My beautiful one, and come! The winter is now past, the rain is over and gone, arise, My love,

My beautiful one, and come!" There was her "Fiat: Behold the handmaid of the Lord." And her soul went forth to its Beloved. Her death was the simple consequence of her love, of the vehement tending to God that bore her to Him when He withdrew the force which kept her here. Sinless though she was, she had to die, that she might be more perfectly conformed to the likeness of her Son.

An ancient legend says that all the Apostles who were then alive were present at her death and burial. All except Thomas. Thomas had refused to believe in the Resurrection till he should have the utmost evidence of sense. Arriving among the Apostles three days after the entombment of our Lady, he expressed the very characteristic desire to see for himself where they had laid the sacred body. They opened the sepulchre and found it empty. But spotless lilies were blooming where the body of Mary Immaculate had been laid. Must not the cry of praise have come to the lips of all: "Thou wilt not suffer Thy holy one to see corruption" (Ps. 15). "She is not here, she is arisen: behold the place where we laid her!"

III. "And on the third day she laid away the garments she wore, and put on her glorious apparel. And glittering in royal robes…she stood before the king where he sat on his royal throne."—Esther xv.

There was mingled joy and sorrow in the hearts of the disciples as they turned away from the death bed of Mary—motherless.

But beyond the veil, what unclouded joy! What bliss through the length and breadth of heaven. What exultation amid the angelic host. What preparations for receiving as their Queen the lowliest of the earth. See them trooping forth in myriads to meet her—Angels and Archangels, Dominations, and Principalities, and Powers, all the Heavenly army. In their midst, the Son of Man, the Son of Mary, His Sacred Heart beating quick with loving expectation as He speeds on His way. Thronging round Him a special escort, Joseph, and Joachim, and Anna, and Eve, and Adam. Our father Abraham, and Moses, and David, and Judith, and Esther.

Hear the Angels and their human brethren inciting each other to the praises of God:

"O ye Angels of the Lord, bless the Lord, praise and exalt Him above all for over (Dan. 3).

"O ye sons of men, bless the Lord, praise and exalt Him above all for ever" (*Id.*).

"Bless the Lord, all ye His Angels…bless the Lord, all ye His hosts" (Ps. 103).

"O ye holy and humble of heart, bless the Lord, praise and exalt Him above all for ever" (Dan. 3).

Hush! "Who is this that cometh up from the desert, Gabriel by her side? Comes with the swiftness of light; comes with the humility of the creature, with the eagerness of a mother, with the majesty of a queen? Oh see her as she falls at His feet; as she adores Him; as she offers herself to Him: "*Ecce ancilla*: Behold the handmaid of the Lord!" See how He raises her and folds her to His Heart. Watch with ecstasy that meeting of the Mother and the Son, the pledge of so many blessed meetings beyond the grave, the reunion that glorifies earth's sweet ties and re-knits them for eternity!

"There was silence in Heaven as it were for half an hour" (Apoc. 8). There is silence all around as the Son folds His Immaculate Mother in an embrace which has to compensate her for pain such as He alone has understood, such as He alone can reward. How she slakes her soul's thirst at the Fount of living water! How she gazes on His glory—and is satisfied!

See Him presenting her to the homage of His Heavenly Court, Queen of Angels and Archangels, Patriarchs and Prophets, Apostles and Martyrs, Confessors and Virgins, Queen of all Saints. Hear as it resounds through space that "*Ave!*" in the Heavens: "Hail, lull of grace, the Lord is with thee! Thou art the glory of Jerusalem: thou art the joy of Israel, thou art the honour of our people!" And Mary says: "My soul doth magnify the Lord, and my spirit hath rejoiced in God my Saviour."

Watch her passing through the Eternal Gates. See the lowliness with which she presents herself before the Throne of the Ever Blessed Trinity. Behold her welcome there. The Eternal Father receives back unsullied from this sinful earth the first and fairest of His creatures. Receives it back, not unsullied only, but in the fulness of perfect beauty: the only soul that returns to His hands with His design respecting it realised with faultless perfection; every gift and grace utilised to the utmost, to His greater glory. See the tenderness with which He blesses this His well-beloved Daughter. Behold the filial reverence with which the Eternal Son welcomes into His Kingdom His Mother who is to sit for ever at His right hand. The ineffable complacency and love with which the Eternal Spirit broods over His Immaculate Spouse.

"Let us be glad and rejoice and give glory to Him" (Apoc. 19). O Ever Blessed Trinity, herein is our joy, that Thou art pleased to joy in Mary. We give Thee thanks for the great glory Thou dost receive, and through eternity shall receive from this perfect work of Thy hands. Glory be to the Father, and to the

Son, and to the Holy Ghost. As it was in the beginning, is now, and ever shall be, world without end. Amen.

>IV. **Thou shall be called My pleasure in her.**—Isaias lxii.

>>Hail to thee, Maid of Nazareth! alone
>>In thy pure beauty. Thou shalt call thine own
>>The co-eternal Son. Bowed low her head,
>>"Behold the handmaid of the Lord," she said,
>>>"His Will be done!"

>>Mother of Sorrows! on the Tree accursed
>>Must hang the tender Child thy bosom nursed,
>>A living death thy lot. "Yea, even so,
>>Blest be the Father's pleasure. In my woe
>>>His Will be done!"

>>Lo! He ascendeth in triumphant state,
>>Leaving thee, Blessed Mother, desolate.
>>"Glory to Him on high and endless praise,
>>Justified in themselves are all His ways,
>>>His Will be done!"

>>"Hearken, O Daughter, and incline thine ear,
>>Past is the winter's frost, the flowers appear,
>>Arise, make haste, and come!" She heard, she sped
>>Whither He called. Still, as His handmaid, said:
>>>"Thy Will be done!"

>>"Life in His Will."[1] Peace in the "Fiat" here,
>>That binds us to our God mid trial and tear;
>>There in the Home above, the "Fiat" still,
>>The joyous revelling in our Father's Will
>>>As it is done in Heaven.

>V. **It is good for me to adhere to my God.**—Ps. lxxii.

See the room where, surrounded by the Apostles and the holy women, her companions, the Mother of God awaits the moment of death.

---

1 Ps. 29.

Every eye is fixed reverently upon her. She has been their teacher, their counsellor, their comforter, their refuge, since the Ascension of her Divine Son. And now the hour has come for her last lesson in this life.

What is that lesson? One that it behoves every creature to learn, from the lowliest to the most exalted; the lesson life is given us to learn; the lesson that renders every death of His saints precious in the sight of God: "It is good for me to adhere to my God."

It is good for me to realise that of myself I am nothing, that my duty, my utility, my safety, my happiness, my glory, consist in my dependence on my Creator—"*Ecce ancilla*, behold the handmaid of the Lord!"

It is good for me to listen for His secret voice in my heart and conscience; to hearken and incline my ear to every word that proceeds from His mouth: "Speak, Lord, for Thy servant heareth: *Ecce ancilla!*"

It is good for me to know by a most intimate conviction that all my good consists in adhering to His Will; in accepting with filial confidence every disposition of His Providence as regards myself or others: "Yea, Father, for so hath it seemed good in Thy sight" (Matth. 11). "*Ecce ancilla!*"

It is good for me to understand and feel that in the trials and difficulties of daily life, no less than in its moments of crisis, my best of friends is my Creator; His bosom my resting-place; His arms my refuge; His strength my safety; His Providence my trust; His love my all in all. "For what have I in Heaven but Thee, and beside Thee what do I desire upon earth" (Ps. 72). "*Ecce ancilla!*"

And if in life, much more in death, it is good for me to cleave to my God, to cling to Him in complete abandonment, in perfect trust. Let me lay myself down in His arms to die. And waking there in the next life, like a child from sleep, let me realise as I look up into His face, realise through a happy eternity, that it was indeed good for me to adhere to my God, to put my trust in the Lord God.

VI. The souls of the just are in the hand of God
and the torment of death shall not touch them.—Wisd. iii.

Death shall touch us every one, but the saints, safe in the hand of God, shall not feel its torment. What is that torment?

Three things are wont to assail and torture the dying:

(1) The remembrance of past sins; of time, and grace, and opportunities lost, and lost—for ever.

(2) The present anguish of mind and body, caused by physical and mental distress; by the coming separation from family, friends, possessions, all the heart holds dear; by the temptations of the Evil One who knows his time is short.

(3) The uncertain future—eternity close at hand; the fear of the judgments of God: "Man knoweth not whether he be worthy of love or of hatred" (Eccles. 9).

This is the "torment" that waits upon the deathbed. What is there to prevent the trembling soul from sinking into despair?

"Underneath are the everlasting arms" (Deut. 33) to sustain, and shield, and shelter it. God has at hand for that hour the grace of His sacraments to allay the torment of death, even to remove it altogether and change it into a foretaste of eternal joy. "Precious in the sight of the Lord is the death of His saints" (Ps. 115). "Blessed are the dead who die in the Lord; from henceforth…they may rest from their labours for their works follow them" (Apoc. 14).

"Their works." We must have done our work if we are to lie down trustfully to our rest in the arms of our Heavenly Father. We must have done our work if we are to expect His recompense. "Work your work before the time and He will give you your reward in His time" (Ecclus. 51). We must have so lived our life that He can make our retrospect as we lie down to die a happy and a hopeful one. We must have washed our robes and made them white in the Blood of the Lamb if we are to be fit to appear before Him. We must have used time, and grace, and opportunity whilst they were ours. God Himself cannot restore them when the end has come. "Walk whilst you have the light, that the darkness overtake you not" (John 12).

We must have schooled ourselves to submission to God's Will in physical and mental trials. We must have been in the world but not of it; held its fleeting goods with a loose hand, and let Him who gave, take away, as it pleased Him.

We must have learned to trust Him with so perfect a reliance during our journey on earth, that we can cast ourselves into His arms with a child's unquestioning faith when He calls us Home. The holiest, safest, most meritorious preparation for death, is this complete abandonment to our Heavenly Father for any disposal He may make of us in time and eternity.

For those who have thus lived in the hand of God during life, death has no terrors, its torment shall not touch them.

> VII. May my soul die the death of the just,
> and my last end be like unto theirs.—Numb. xxiii.

My God, I commend to Thy Fatherly keeping the most momentous hour of my life, the hour on which eternity hangs—the hour of my death.

Let it come when Thou seest me best prepared. Let it come with that time for preparation which Thou seest best, and attended by the circumstances which Thou who knowest my need shalt appoint—so much of physical pain, of temptation, of mental suffering as will be for my greater good, and no more; so much spiritual assistance and consolation as will profit me.

If, as I hope, Thou hast in store for me the last succours of the Church, let me bring to them such preparation as will enable me to draw from them abundant fruit. Let me leave nothing to be said in my last confession, but put all straight with Thee now. Help me in my last hour to make an act of perfect contrition—of sorrow because I have dishonoured and wronged Thee, my Father, by the sins of my life.

I shall be very weak then and wandering, weary, and in pain of body and mind. I cannot expect, dear Lord, that my preparation for receiving Thee in Holy Communion for the last time will be better than it is now when I am in health. Accept what I shall be able to give Thee. Help me to make my acts of faith and hope and charity, of humility and desire. Help me in my thanksgiving. Come to me then with all the help I shall need for the last passage—faith to hold fast all that Thy Church teaches; trust to cling fast to Thee in spite of the terrifying sight of my sins; patience to take from Thy hand all the pains and sorrows of death; confidence to cast myself into Thy arms for time and eternity, trusting to Thy Sacred Heart the sentence that is to decide my eternal lot.

Prepare me Thyself for the last holy anointing. Purify my soul from the last relics of sin by the touch of Thy Church in Extreme Unction. Forgive me all my misuse of my senses throughout my life.

Let me benefit to the full by the Last Blessing and Plenary Indulgence. Put into my soul so deep a sorrow for my sins that the whole temporal punishment they have deserved may be remitted.

And then, when the Church has laid her hand upon me for the last time, and is giving me up into Thy hands, receive me, O my Saviour, with loving-kindness and with mercy. May my trembling soul depart in the safe keeping of Thy holy Mother, under the protection of Michael, "the prince of all the souls to be received," and of my holy Angel Guardian. Thus let me be brought into Thy presence. Thus let me look up into Thy face, and hear Thee say: "Come, blessed of My Father, come!"

VIII. God will show His brightness in thee, to every one under heaven.—Baruch v.

(1) Thou shalt no more have the sun for thy light by day, neither shall the brightness of the moon enlighten thee, for the Lord shall be unto thee for an everlasting light, and thy God for thy glory (Isaias 60).

(2) Thou shalt be a crown of glory in the hand of the Lord, and a royal diadem in the hand of thy God (Isaias 62).

(3) Go in to the King, and entreat Him for thy people. Who knoweth whether thou art not therefore come to the kingdom that thou mightest be ready in such a time as this? (Esther 4).

(4) Do thou speak to the King for us, and deliver us from death (Esther 15).

(5) And she said to the King: I desire one small petition of Thee. And the King said to her: My Mother ask for I must not turn away thy face (III. Kings 2).

(6) She spoke to Him all that she had in her heart…And the King gave her all that she desired and asked of Him (III. Kings 10).

The Coronation of the Blessed Virgin in Heaven

I. And the King arose to meet her, and bowed to her, and sat down upon his throne, and a throne was set for the King's mother, and she sat on his right hand.—3 Kings ii.

And a great sign appeared in heaven, a woman clothed with the sun, and the moon under her feet, and on her head a crown of twelve stars.—Apoc. xii.

SEE the meek majesty of Mary, as with hands folded on her breast, she bends before her Son to receive her crown.
See the filial reverence, the content, the joy with which He crowns His chosen Mother and seats her on His right hand.

See the profound homage paid her by the Court of Heaven. And hear her humble explanation of it all: "He that is mighty hath done great things to me, and holy is His name."

The heavenly Jerusalem is glorious beyond all that the richest imagination can conceive, with its foundations of precious stones, its gates of pearl, its streets of pure gold; with the river of the water of life clear as crystal, proceeding from the throne of God and of the Lamb, and on both sides of the river the tree of life. No need of sun or moon to shine on it, for the glory of God enlightens it and the Lamb is the lamp thereof. A great multitude which no man could number, of all nations and tribes and peoples and tongues stand before the throne, clothed in white robes and palms in their hands. Thousands of thousands minister to Him who sits upon the throne, and a hundred times a hundred thousand stand before Him (Dan. 7).

What must a coronation be in that glorious city! What was the glory of that diadem of stars with which the Queen of Angels was crowned by her Son, the King of Kings!

Who crowns? The just Judge who will render to every man according to his works, and who finds every thought, word, and work of Mary throughout a long life deserving of the highest recompense. He crowns who is her Son as well as her Judge, and whose filial Heart thrills with joy at the magnificence of the reward He is able to bestow.

Who is crowned? The lowliest of earth's children; the work of His hands as one of us; an hour ago an exile mourning and weeping in this valley of tears. One who has never disappointed Him; who has glorified Him perfectly from the first moment of her existence; who has dedicated her whole being to Him with a generosity that reserved nothing for self; who has taken His Will for the rule of her life even to its least details. One to whom has been confided the highest dignity that God Himself could bestow on a creature, and who has proved herself worthy of His confidence.

What is crowned in Mary? This faultless fidelity; faith, hope, and charity, by which she has adhered to God with ever-growing strength and affection; humility that at a height which places her in the most intimate relations with the God of Heaven and earth, sees nothing in herself but the handmaid of the Lord; patience that the weight of her cross never wearied; perseverance that sustained the heroism of every virtue up to the end.

How is Mary crowned? With a glory corresponding with her dignity, her merit, her office in the Kingdom of God. All that God can communicate of His riches, He makes over to her freely—unparalleled exaltation, universal sovereignty, the dispensation of His treasures, omnipotent intercession with Himself. "My Mother, ask, for I must not turn away thy face" (III. Kings 2). "And the King gave the queen all that she desired and asked of Him, besides what He offered her of Himself of His royal bounty" (III. Kings 10). He gave her the homage and service of Angels, who, from the lowest to the highest, glory in their subjection to their human Queen. He gives her consolation and joy for every sorrow she has suffered for His sake. And such abounding joy that we have no thoughts to think it. If it hath not entered into the heart of man to conceive what God has prepared for such as we are, how should we be able to rise to the comprehension of Mary's joy! She herself has no words tor it. She can only say: "He that is mighty hath done great things to me."

He who crowned the Mother is waiting to crown the children. To us too He is the just Judge who will render to every one according to his works. Do these words awake fear rather than hope in us who are conscious of our sinfulness and know not whether we are worthy of love or of hatred? We must not wrong God by taking a one-sided view of His justice. He rewards in eternity all He can find to reward. He shows His justice by remembering—not our failings only—as the enemy and our fearful hearts would have us believe, but the least little things in which He can discover a particle of good. He who crowns is not our Judge only but our Father and our Friend, whom no good thought, word, work, or desire has ever escaped, and who has treasured up all against the day of reward. He crowns who often and often discerns merit where we see nothing but failure and fault, because while we consider results, He looks solely at the good will and the effort. He crowns who, precisely because he is just, is merciful and indulgent. For He knoweth our frame. "His eyes see our imperfect being" (Ps. 138). "He remembereth that we are dust" (Ps. 102).

What am I getting ready for Him to crown?

> II. They shall see the Son of Man coming in the clouds of heaven with much power and majesty.—Matth. xxiv.

In the Rosary I look back on scenes that are past. If I have a place therein it is by thought and affection only. But in the last mystery I may look forward to a scene in the future in which I shall be intimately concerned, in which I shall take part, not in thought only, but personally, body and soul. As truly as Mary stood on Calvary at the Crucifixion, and the Apostles on Olivet at the Ascension, shall I stand in the valley of Jehoshaphat on the last day to await my Judge. "Come, all ye nations from round about, and gather yourselves together. Let them arise and come up into the valley of Jehoshaphat, for there I will sit to judge all nations" (Joel 3).

I will go thither in spirit now and behold the preparations for Judgment.

There have been disturbances in the heavens, in the air, in the sea. The earth, swept by a devouring fire, is reduced to a charred, black mass—churches, libraries, theatres, the palaces and the slums of great cities—all destroyed. Heaps of ashes and the silence of the grave where the world's turmoil and traffic was. "Merchandise of gold and silver and precious stones, and of pearls, and of fine linen…and odours and ointment, and wine, and oil, and wheat, and beasts, and sheep, and horses, and chariots…all goodly things are perished and shall be found no more at all in her. And the voice of musicians shall no more be heard at all in her; and no craftsman of any art whatsoever shall he found any more at all in her, and the sound of the mill shall be heard no more at all in her. And the light of the lamp shall shine no more at all in her, and the voice of the bridegroom and the bride shall be heard no more at all in her" (Apoc. 18). Created things have done their work. They were made for the service of man. God's servants have used them well, sinners ill. All are now called to give an account of their stewardship.

I hear the blast of the Archangel's trumpet: "Arise, ye dead and come to Judgment." As lightning flashing from west to east, souls speed from heaven, purgatory, hell, to seek in the graves of earth and in the sea their companions of long ago, the bodies in which they worked out their salvation or their ruin. I see the meeting of the souls and bodies of the elect and of the reprobate. In the twinkling of an eye all are transported to the valley of Jehoshaphat for the final scene of the world's history. What meetings there, and what separations, as the Angels part into two companies the millions of the human race, to stand on the right hand and on the left of the Judge. I shall be there. Where will be my place? Angels and saints know my lot before my Judge appears.

I see the astonishment of men to find the world destroyed: their estimate of its grandeurs and its pleasures now. Behind them to the west is Calvary where their Redemption was wrought. Above, in the clouds, the Throne of the Judge.

The heavens part. The procession comes forth. In a flood of blinding light appears the Sign of the Son of Man, borne by Angels. The upturned faces of men reflect its glory. Our Lord appears, His Wounds shining as the sun. His Blessed Mother as Queen. All mankind without exception fall prostrate before Him and adore the Sacred Humanity. They rise and look upon Him whom they have pierced.

I hear the cry of joy of the elect as they are caught up into the clouds to meet Him. He seats Himself upon the Throne of His Majesty. Each human being stands before Him and is judged by Him. Every thought, word, and deed, however hidden, is laid bare before the whole world; the terrors of that Day, the vast multitudes arraigned, the concern of every one for himself, not distracting any from the manifestation of each. I see the agonising shame of the wicked; of those who did not dare to confess their sins in life; the consolation and joy of the just who have washed their robes in the Blood of the Lamb and now appear spotless in His sight. The good is published as well as the bad. All the virtue of the saints, every victory over temptation, every act of meekness, self-denial, kindness to the suffering members and to the little ones of Christ, every secret prayer and good desire—all is revealed.

I hear Our Lord giving sentence: "Come ye Blessed. Depart ye cursed." I see the despair of those who are banished for ever from the company of Christ and His saints; how they depart weeping and wailing into everlasting fire. I see clearly how in losing God they have lost all. I share the transports of joy with which the saints behold the triumph of their Lord so long delayed. Yonder lay the city where He was mocked and tortured for them, the Mount where he was crucified for them. I see the dazzling beauty of so many glorified bodies; the delight of the saints in the agility, subtlety, brightness, that now belong to them. I hear the rejoicing, the congratulations on every side; the songs of exultation and praise as they mount into the heavens, higher and higher: "Alleluia. Salvation, and glory, and power is to our God. For true and just are His judgments. Alleluia. The Lord our God, the Almighty hath reigned. Let us be glad and rejoice and give glory to Him, for the marriage of the Lamb is come" (Apoc. 19).

The Eternal Gates open before them. They pass in with Jesus and Mary. Shall I be there? The Gates are shut. O God, on which side shall I be? The choice remains with me now. By every act of my life I am choosing my place for eternity.

O Mother of God and my Mother, pray for me now. Thy prayer on that Day would be too late. Whatever happens to me in this life, I must, I must secure my eternity in the next with Thy Divine Son and with thee. Pray for me that I may not be lost in the dreadful Judgment. Let all things go—pleasures, companions, self-indulgence, worldly position, anything and everything that would endanger my salvation.

III. "Come, ye blessed of My Father, possess you the kingdom prepared for you from the foundation of the world."—Matth. xxv.

What a joyous life begins when the Gates of their Home close behind the children of God! Without, across the gulf, crouches the deadly foe who pursued them with unrelenting hate up to the moment of death. He is chained. He is conquered. He will never trouble them more. No more temptation or fear. No more evil tendencies. No more conflict without or within. The former things are passed away. They have fought the good fight. The day of triumph and reward is come.

Into what a glorious company we are admitted! See the meetings! Hear the congratulations! The Angels who have never known the taint of sin, are welcoming with brotherly affection those who have washed their robes in the Blood of the Lamb, and who are now their companions, their worthy companions, for eternity. How wondrously the gifts of immortality, agility, subtlety, brightness, have transfigured "the body of our lowliness"! Are these the same bodies in which our salvation was laboriously worked out, which were such a clog to us on earth? The transformation of the crawling caterpillar into the gorgeous butterfly, of the bare wintry landscape into the glories of summer foliage and flower, is a poor figure of the change the Resurrection has wrought in the bodies of the saints. Of indescribable and infinitely varied loveliness, I see they are all conformed to their Prototype, the Risen Body of Christ. I understand now what He meant when He said: "He that eateth My Flesh and drinketh My Blood, hath everlasting life: and I will raise him up in the last day" (John. 6). Oh why did I not think oftener in my Communions of that pledge of eternal life which He gave me in giving me Himself!

But the change in the soul is more wondrous still. All its powers are renovated, perfected, satisfied. Whatever can give happiness in the remembrance of the past, in looking back on our lives, in the recollection of what God has done for us, and of what we have done for Him, is present to the memory without effort, as a delicious fount of joy. Whatever would overcloud the soul's happiness even for an instant, is banished from its remembrance for ever. All darkness and dulness in the understanding has vanished like a cloud before the sun. We see our God. We are face to face with the Eternal Truth. We know even as we are known. The pleasure that comes from the full development of the noblest faculty of our soul and its employment on the Infinite God, is indescribable. Our minds are keen, eager, strong. And they penetrate the deep things of God with an ever-growing wonder and delight.

And the will—what a change there! No more sluggishness, no more coldness, no more distraction. To look on God is to be drawn to Him with all the soul's vehemence and power of love. Every affection centres in Him with whom we have but one will, in the calm thrilling enjoyment of whom we are at rest. Oh that rest in the Bosom of God; that peace, that security in the possession of Him whom we love with every fibre of our being, of Him who made us for Himself, from whom nothing can ever separate us! Is not this untiring energy and activity of all our powers, this tranquil repose and contentment of all—Life indeed! How poor compared with Life Eternal was that existence we called life awhile ago!

God is my Father, and He makes me feel I am in very truth His child. He makes me welcome to all the delights of my Home. "Take all, child. See, hear, enjoy all without fear. The days of restraint are past. All is for you. The more you enjoy what I have prepared for you from eternity, the more you will please and glorify Me." How can I help enjoying where all is perfect and delightful beyond anything I could have conceived. All that can charm the senses is here. The sounds, the sights, the fragrant scents of my Home, how sweet they are! On every side songs of praise are rising to the Throne of God. And in the ravishing harmony I distinguish the dear, familiar voices silenced so long ago on earth, and, as it seemed, for ever.

How miserable would the most gorgeous pageants of earth appear beside the grand sights of Heaven! These thousands of thousands of blessed spirits. These countless hosts of saints. What joy to carry on in eternity the friendship with them begun on earth. To meet our Patron Saints, not now as Patrons, but as dear brothers and sisters in our Father's House, all rejoicing in our happiness, all so glad we are come. And the marvellous charity everywhere! Not one in this vast multitude but breaks forth into fresh praise of God for my company, and calls on me to join my voice with theirs and take up my part in the unending songs of jubilee. But if the sight of all the blessed brings such joy, what is it to meet my Angel Guardian, so happy at the success of his long labour of love, so delighted in my delight! O dear Angel, can you forgive and forget my forgetfulness and waywardness in the past? What happiness to meet in a blessed eternity those who were bound to me by special ties on earth: to find the old home reconstructed in the great Home where all shall be reunited in everlasting joy before the Face of our Father who is in Heaven!

One of the surprises of Heaven is to feel so completely at ease in the midst of such magnificent sanctity. I keep forgetting that I am no more what I was; that the glorious change I see in others, they see with delight in me. I am worthy—oh, can it be really true!—of the companionship of Angels and saints. And here are none of earth's formalities and constraints in treating with those in loftier stations than ourselves. Though in our Father's House there are many mansions, we are free to go in and out as we will, welcome everywhere, everywhere the objects of an overflowing affection that has utterly taken me by surprise. Wherever we go we are at Home. And the higher we ascend the more easy of access we find our blessed companions.

I kneel at Mary's feet. I feel her hand resting on my shoulder. I look into her face and meet her smile, and know my Mother understands all I would say. At last I can love and thank her as she deserves.

Higher still. I fall at the feet of Jesus. I adore Him with all the intensity of worship, love, and gratitude of which I am capable now. He raises me with tender words, and I dare to lift my eyes and look upon Him. This is He who became incarnate for me, who died for me; whom at prayer, and in the silence of the night, and as I gazed upon the white Host in the monstrance I have tried to picture to myself. For the first time I see the Human Face of Jesus. His eyes look down into mine. What that first glance of His has said! It has told me how dear I am to Him, how happy He is to have me safe with Him at last. He lays His wounded Hands upon my head. He speaks to me. I hear the tones of the Voice that thrilled to their depths the souls of Mary, and Joseph, and Peter, and Magdalen, and John. What are all the songs of Heaven compared with the music of that Voice! How sweet He is, how gracious, how attractive! Who would think that Infinite Majesty could be so tender? That He who knows me through and through, knows how I have served Him, how miserably I have corresponded with His Grace, could treat me like this! He thanks me for every little thing I have ever done for Him, things I had forgotten, things that seem beneath His notice. I look up at Him through such happy tears. "Lord, dost Thou thank *me*? Oh if the past years were to come over again, there should be a difference in my service and in my love! Why was not all my service love of Thee!

Higher still. All this excess of glory and happiness, this beauty and splendour, this delightful companionship with Angels and Saints, this reunion with those we love—all this is not the essential bliss of Heaven, but a mere accessory, the additional joy which comes to the Blessed from creatures. The essential happiness is that which the soul receives immediately from God in the Beatific Vision, that happy-making sight which banishes all pain and sorrow and infuses eternal joy. As children of God, one thing alone can content us when the mists of this world are swept away—the Face of our Father who is in Heaven. Even in this life, even before the Incarnation had revealed our Father to us as it has done, the cry of the human heart was for that Face. "I have sought Thy Face…Turn not away Thy Face from me" (Ps. 26). "Cast me not away from Thy Face" (Ps. 50). "Thou shalt fill me with joy with Thy countenance" (Ps. 15).

The babe in its mother's arms looks up into her face and is content. Now and again she plays with it, hiding her face. But if the hiding lasts, if the veil does not quickly drop, there will be wailing cries.

O my Heavenly Father—Father, Mother, all in all to me, I the least of Thy children, I too long to see Thy Face. However my heart has been stained and spoilt, however far it has wandered from Thee, it is the heart of Thy child still. "Show me Thy Face" (Cant. 2). "When shall I appear before the Face of God?" (Ps. 41).

IV. These that are clothed in white robes, who are they, and whence came they?—Apoc. vii.

Who are these without spot before the throne of God?

Souls that awhile ago were struggling with temptation and with sin. That were full of imperfections. That had their strivings and their falls, their good and bad days, their disappointments, their discouragements. There were times when Heaven seemed so distant and shadowy as to be almost unreal. And the interests of time were pressing, and the world and the things of sense were all but overpowering in their claims.

But Faith kept us safe. We saw dimly, indeed; through a glass in a dark manner. But we did see. And what we saw we hoped for. The sight of our Home lured us on. We shook ourselves free from what was entangling us, and set our faces steadfastly to go to Jerusalem.

And here we are at last! Faith did not deceive us. It was all true that she showed. But was that true and real which so nearly ensnared us? Seen from this height, in the light of Truth, it looks so thin and vague and unattractive, that we can scarcely believe it could once have been a danger.

V. What I do thou knowest not now but thou shalt know hereafter.—John xiii.

One of the joys awaiting us in Heaven is to hear from the lips of our Lord Himself, as we kneel at His feet, the secrets of His dealings with us in the past. "The judgements of the Lord are true, justified in themselves." (Ps. 18). What He does needs no justification. It must always be right, always the best for us. If we are loyal to Him this is as clear to us as the sun at noon. Yet, with all our trust, we look forward to the fulfilment of His promise: "What I do thou knowest not now but thou shalt know hereafter." The day comes when He deigns to explain to us His mysterious ways with us in life. Why the cross was not lifted though we prayed so earnestly and so long. Why a grace that seemed necessary was refused us, and plans that concerned His glory went unblessed.

He reminds us how the sisters at Bethany sent to Him in their distress. "Lord, he whom Thou lovest is sick." No petition, but a message, every word of which spoke of trust more powerful than any pleading. It went straight to His Heart. Yet He left them in their sorrow and desolation. And their brother died. Not even then did He go to comfort them. In loneliness and heaviness of heart, and not a little wonder at the Master's ways, they followed their dead to the grave. And went back to the desolate home and began their days of mourning. Then He came to them. His disciples who knew His love for that little household had marvelled too at His delay. And still more at His words to them: "I am glad for your sakes that I was not there."

Our Lord's friends knew the tenderness of His Heart. And thus it was that when at last He came, both sisters as they fell at His feet told Him in the same words that had He been with them and seen their pain, their brother's death simply could not have happened.

He owns to this Himself. "I am glad for your sakes that I was not there," He had said to the Apostles. Glad because of the gain to their faith by the resurrection of Lazarus, and because of the exercise of faith, confidence, and patience on the part of Martha and Mary. But He speaks as if He could not have trusted His Heart in the sorrowing household: "I am glad for your sakes that I was not there." Even when the hour of consolation was come, when in a few moments the brother they mourned would be restored to them, even then their tears drew forth His own. "Jesus, therefore, when He had seen her weeping, and the Jews weeping also, troubled Himself in spirit ...And Jesus wept."

"I am glad for your sakes." So will He say to us in the hour when His hand shall wipe away all tears from our eyes. "O child, I am glad now of all the distress there has been in the past; of the hours of patient suffering, and waiting, and disappointment; of the pain in partings; of the broken-hearted sorrow beside the grave. I am glad that in view of this hour of recompense I did violence to My pity and My love, restraining both that your heart may rejoice now with exceeding great joy, that according to the multitude of sorrows in your heart My comforts may give joy to your soul" (Ps. 93).

VI. "*Requiescat in pace.*"

"May they rest in peace," is the prayer of Mother Church for us when life here is done. "May he rest in peace," as she turns away from the deathbed that she has tended, and soothed, and sanctified up to the last; as she commits to the earth the body that is to be held in trust for the Resurrection. "May he rest in peace," as she follows the soul on its journey to the Judgment seat and pleads for it there. "May they rest in peace," as she gazes wistfully after her children from her altars, and in every hour of her office, remembering them long, long, perchance, after their dearest on earth have forgotten them.

What is this peace that she bespeaks for us? For the body it is the well-earned repose after the burden and heat of the day through which it has toiled in the Master's service. It is the consignment to earth of the grain that must die before rising again to its new and proper life.

And the soul—where is its rest? Where but in the Bosom of God whence it came. He must pillow it there or it will throb and ache with torturing pain, with the ceaseless craving of unsatisfied desire, for the term of its separation from Him, or for ever. "Thou hast made us for Thyself O Lord, and our heart is restless until it rests in Thee."

May the soul rest in peace upon the Bosom of God even here? Can it amid this scene of turmoil and unceasing change lie there in security, untossed, untroubled? Not with the freedom from fear and sorrow that awaits it hereafter, not with the fulness of joy that is to be its portion when the Father's arms close over it for ever and shield it from the least passing breath of ill. Not, then, with "the abundance of peace" which is to come.

Yet even in this life it may truly rest in peace, for the God of peace is its portion, its refuge, its home even now. Even now we may cast our care on Him so unreservedly, trust Him so fully, abandon ourselves to Him so entirely, that the cares and disappointments, the bereavements, all the physical and mental trials of this changeful life will not disturb our rest. They may be surface troubles, or they may pierce to the quick and leave a life-long wound. None the less, the deepest depth of our soul where its vital and most secret energies are stored, may be at peace, for like Deicola who ever smiled we may say: "No one can take my God from me."

Of his fourteen Epistles St. Paul begins all but one with the salutation: "Grace to you and peace from God our Father." His great heart was ever in closest sympathy with those it loved, weak with the weak, weeping with those in sorrow. It was not one to mock the sorely tried by wishing then, a gift beyond their reach. But he sees nothing in their life of outward persecution and inward strife that need disturb their peace. Writing to his converts in Rome who were in the very furnace of tribulation—"famine, persecution, the sword," he says: "Now the God of peace be with you all. Amen" (Rom 15).

VII. "Well done, good and faithful servant!"—Matth. xxv.

The longest life in the service of God is well repaid at last by those words: "Well done!" Or rather there is no proportion at all between the most protracted service, fifty years of the most heroic sacrifice, and the recompense—those words from the lips of Christ. Whatever happens to me in this life, whatever else of consolation or of happiness I may miss, may I not miss those words when life is done.

What must I do, Lord, to deserve this welcome from Thee at the last?

One essential condition is to remember and thoroughly realize that it has to be deserved. It is not enough to desire, I must deserve. Five virgins out of ten were ready to cry out: "Lord, Lord, open to us! But the preparation was wanting." Their lamps had gone out. And the answer to their knocking and their cry was: "Amen, I say to you, I know you not."

How dost Thou know us, Divine Bridegroom, so as to admit us to Thy presence?

Thou knowest the careful trimming of the lamp in spite of the weariness of monotony and delay. Thou knowest the fidelity of love that through hours of darkness watches on in silence and in hope. Thou knowest the regularity in religious duties that does not look for sweetness and consolation as its pay; the diligence that works cheerfully and conscientiously because it works for Thee; the courage that without the sustaining force of example holds on its course.

Those who watch thus are ready at Thy coming. They meet Thee joyfully. They go with Thee to the marriage. They hear from Thy lips "Well done!"

> Thou, who a lowly bride to woo and gain
> A treasury of love divine wouldst drain,
> A human lot embrace, weep human tears,
> Have fellowship with me in hopes and fears,
> Toil at my side, a daily burden bear,
> Nor quivering flesh, nor quailing spirit spare;
> Planing, Thy feet, where'er my feet have trod,
> Lifting, Thy lever-life, my life to God:

> Where, Lord and Bridegroom, where the guerdon won
> At such stupendous cost? Hath fraud undone
> Thine expectation, dared Thy suit to thwart,
> And Lia proffer, for the Rachel sought?
> Long years of labour as a single day
> Thy love hath counted: have they borne away
> The prize on which Thy faithful Heart is set,
> Or is my strange, dull heart unconquered yet?

> O Christ, sole Lover that may love constrain,
> Abandon not, nor let Thy quest be vain;
> By Bethlehem's joys, by Calvary's bitter death,
> By the sweet memories of Nazareth,
> Give me the lesson of Thy life to learn;
> Give me the love that would Thy love return:
> Though cold my heart, unworthy, selfish, small,
> Have patience with me till I pay Thee all!

VIII. "I have loved thee with an everlasting love, therefore have I drawn thee taking pity on thee."—Jer. xxxi.

I. Who is it that has drawn me?
II. Whence has He drawn me?
III. Whither is He drawing me?

I. God, the Almighty, the All Wise, the All Good, who infinitely happy in Himself, is also infinitely liberal, and desires to make others, to make me a sharer in His happiness—He it is that draws me.

To this end He created my soul out of nothing and gave it a likeness to Himself that it might be capable of participating in His blessedness. This likeness is in the natural order, because by its three powers my soul resembles Him in His Three Persons. Still more is it in the supernatural order by the gift of sanctifying grace which makes my soul a sharer in the Divine Nature, a child of God, having a distinct right to call him Father.

This grace given in Baptism is increased in every Sacrament, and it is always in the Name of the Most Holy Trinity that it is bestowed.

The priest's words to us at our Baptism were: "I baptize thee in the Name of the Father, and of the Son, and of the Holy Ghost." When we were confirmed the bishop said: "I confirm thee…in the Name of the Father, and of the Son and of the Holy Ghost." As children of God we have in a sense a right to the children's Bread in which we receive the Giver of grace Himself, Jesus Christ, with whom are present by circumincession the Father and the Holy Ghost. If by mortal sin we lose grace, it is in the Name of the Blessed Trinity that it is restored to us: "I absolve thee from thy sins in the Name of the Father, and of the Son, and of the Holy Ghost."

And when at last the end shall come, and Holy Church has to pour out all her treasures to strengthen us for our passage into the life beyond the grave, it is again in the Name of the Most Holy Trinity that she gives us the Sacrament of Extreme Unction: "In the Name of the Father, and of the Son, and of the Holy Ghost," the priest will say, "may all the power of the devil be extinguished in thee by the imposition of our hands."

More tenderly still the Church will commend our departing soul to God: "Go forth, O Christian soul, from this world, in the Name of the Father Almighty who created thee, in the Name of Jesus Christ, the Son of the living God, who suffered for thee, in the Name of the Holy Ghost who was poured out upon thee." And again: "We commend to Thee, O Lord, the soul of Thy servant N…For although he hath sinned he hath not denied the Father and the Son and the Holy Ghost."

"Go forth." What daring words. Yet why should it fear to go, that Christian soul, so loved by Cod, so compassed throughout its course by graces! Why should not the Church break forth into a song of triumph over her weak trembling child, even in the hour when all is failing it! Why should she not summon to meet and welcome it Angels and Archangels, Apostles, white-robed Martyrs, Confessors crowned with lilies, the choir of Virgins singing jubilees! Is this too much for me? No, for I am a child of the Church and when my time is come I have a right to pass from the Church Militant and Suffering to the Church Triumphant. I have a right to see at last and know Him in whom I have believed. That His Countenance should be mild and festive when I appear before him, and that He should award me a place among those that are to stand before Him for ever. That He should place me within the ever-verdant gardens of His Paradise. That He, the true Shepherd, should acknowledge me for one of His sheep, and place me at His right hand in the lot of His elect. I have a right to behold my Redeemer face to face, and standing always in His Presence to gaze with blessed eyes on the open Vision of Truth. And set thus among the troops of the Blessed, to enjoy the sweetness of Divine contemplation for ever and ever.

All this is my right as a child of the Church—if only I persevere to the end as her faithful child. It is my right and the Justice of God will award it to me. But I must so live that His Justice may be able to bestow it on me. Now is the time of His Mercy. Now He will give me all manner of good things to which I have no right. But at death this sovereignty of Mercy ceases. He must be just then, just only. Whatever in His Justice He can give me, I shall have. Oh let me make such good use of His Mercy now that I may be able to bear, nay that I may gladly welcome whatever His Justice may decree for me hereafter!

IX. We are the children of Saints and look for that life which God will give to those that never change their faith from Him.—Tobias ii.

(1) I saw a great multitude which no man could number, of all nations, and tribes, and peoples, and tongues, standing before the throne and in sight of the Lamb, clothed with white robes, and palms in their hands (Apoc. 7).

(2) They shall be His people, and God Himself with them shall be their God. And God shall wipe away all tears from their eyes: and death shall be no more, nor mourning, nor crying, nor sorrow shall be any more, for the former things are passed away (Apoc. 21).

(3) The small and great are there (Job 3).

(4) There the wicked cease from troubling, and the wearied are at rest (Job 3).

(5) Alleluia shall be sung in its streets (Tobias 13).

(6) Many are the afflictions of the just but out of them all will the Lord deliver them (Ps. 33).

(7) My elect shall not labour in vain (Isaias 65).

(8) Eye hath not seen, nor ear heard, neither hath it entered into the heart of man what things God hath prepared for them that love Him (I. Cor. 2).

(9) Afflicted in few things in many they shall be well rewarded, because God hath tried them and found them worthy of Himself (Wisd. 3).

(10) Then we set forward…to go to Jerusalem, and the hand of our God was upon us and delivered us from the hand of the enemy and of such as lay in wait by the way. And we came to Jerusalem (Esdras 8).

Additional titles available from
St. Augustine Academy Press
Books for the Traditional Catholic

Titles by Mother Mary Loyola:
Blessed are they that Mourn
Confession and Communion
Coram Sanctissimo (Before the Most Holy)
First Communion
First Confession
Forgive us our Trespasses
Hail! Full of Grace
Heavenwards
Holy Mass/How to Help the Sick and Dying
Home for Good
Jesus of Nazareth: The Story of His Life Written for Children
Questions on First Communion
The Child of God: What comes of our Baptism
The Children's Charter
The Little Children's Prayer Book
The Soldier of Christ: Talks before Confirmation
Trust
Welcome! Holy Communion Before and After

Titles by Father Lasance:
The Catholic Girl's Guide
The Young Man's Guide

Tales of the Saints:
A Child's Book of Saints by William Canton
A Child's Book of Warriors by William Canton
Legends & Stories of Italy by Amy Steedman
Mary, Help of Christians by Rev. Bonaventure Hammer
Page, Esquire and Knight by Marion Florence Lansing
The Book of Saints and Heroes by Leonora Lang
Saint Patrick: Apostle of Ireland
The Story of St. Elizabeth of Hungary by William Canton

Check our Website for more:
www.staugustineacademypress.com

The Seat of Wisdom Series

Learn the lesser-known traditional teachings of our Faith
An excellent supplement to any catechesis program!

by Mother Mary St. Peter

of the Society of the Holy Child Jesus
originally published between 1905 and 1910

Mary the Queen:
A Life of the Blessed Mother for her Little Ones

The Lessons of the King:
Parables Made Plain for His Little Ones

Talks with the Little Ones about the Apostle's Creed

The Queen's Festivals:
An Explanation of the Feasts of the Blessed Virgin Mary

The Story of the Friends of Jesus

The Story of the Miracles of Our Lord

The Gift of the King:
A Simple Explanation of the Doctrines & Ceremonies
of the Holy Sacrifice of the Mass

The Laws of the King:
Talks on the Commandments

"The Sisters of the Holy Child in America have made a distinctly valuable contribution to religious literature for children. There are nearly a dozen neatly printed and illustrated volumes...which are, like Mother Loyola's books, a real joy and help to the child."
—The Ecclesiastical Review, July 1910.

"[Mother Mary St. Peter] has a very clear, pleasing style; and she knows youthful hearts thoroughly. Her talks about the Commandments are excellent, not saying too much, and showing a great deal of shrewdness and discretion in her way of putting things. We are sure that the whole series, of which this is the newest volume, must be very useful for those who are responsible for the instruction of the young."
—The Irish Monthly, July 1910.

www.ingramcontent.com/pod-product-compliance
Lightning Source LLC
LaVergne TN
LVHW011416080426
835512LV00005B/89